Serial Publications
in the British
Parliamentary
Papers
1900-1968

Serial Publications

in the British Parliamentary Papers

1900-1968

A Bibliography

Frank Rodgers

Director of the Library, Portland State University

American Library Association

Chicago 1971

International Standard Book Number 0-8389-0086-0 (1971)

Library of Congress Catalog Card Number 74-117628

Printed in the United States of America

Contents

Acknowledgments

The work which prompted the development of this bibliography was Mrs. Ruby Lane Taylor's *Guide to the Serial and Periodical Publications in Great Britain. Parliament. Sessional Papers. 1914-1933,* issued as the John Crerar Library's Reference List no. 30. I must thank Mr. Herman H. Henkle, former executive director of the John Crerar Library, for granting permission to make use of Mrs. Taylor's material.

Many friends and colleagues have assisted with helpful criticism and valuable suggestions, and I wish to express my particular appreciation to Mrs. Christine R. Longstreet, of the University of Chicago Library, and Mr. William H. Patch, of the University of Wisconsin Library. Their careful reading of the manuscript and their thorough knowledge of its subject matter were responsible for major improvements.

Most of the work was completed at the Pennsylvania State University Libraries. In order to consult examples of all the documents listed, however, it was necessary to use the facilities of several libraries; reference was made to the holdings of the Pennsylvania State Library, the University of Pennsylvania Libraries, the New York Public Library, the British Information Services Library, and some others. I am grateful for the unfailing patience and helpfulness of their staffs.

I must also acknowledge my immense debt to my faithful secretaries, both at the Pennsylvania State University and at Portland State University, without whose typing skills this work would probably still remain unpublished.

Introduction

The purpose of this bibliography is to list by issuing agency all serials which have appeared in the House of Commons Sessional Papers at any time during the present century and to indicate briefly their publishing history: earliest and latest dates of issue, relationship to other publications, and details of non-parliamentary publication when this occurs. It also provides a key to the subject headings used in the principal indexes of parliamentary papers, so that users may easily refer to specific papers or series.

Description of the Sessional Papers

Although most users of this bibliography will probably be well acquainted with the Sessional Papers, a brief description of their arrangement and of the standard form of reference to them may be of value. The arrangement of the documents issued by the House of Commons is based on a system begun in 1801. Each document is numbered as issued, and there are three distinct series:

1. *Public Bills,* numbered serially each session. The numbering on the Bills and in citations is given in parentheses.

2. *Papers,* numbered serially each session. These include a wide variety of Parliamentary Committee reports as well as departmental reports and accounts. When cited, the paper numbers are given in parentheses, but they appear without parentheses on the papers themselves.

3. *Command Papers,* which in theory are issued by command of the Sovereign, but in fact are produced on the initiative of Ministers in

order to inform the House of the work of their departments. They are numbered in a separate series unrelated to the session. The numbers of the first series were printed in brackets to distinguish them from the Bills and Sessional Papers. The second and later series were given letter prefixes. Although the brackets thus became unnecessary, they nevertheless continued to appear on the papers until 1922 and in the indexes until 1950. Each series normally continues until its numbering approaches 10,000.

The five series of Command Papers and their letter prefixes are:

First series	[1]-[4222]	1833-1869
Second series	[C.1]-[C.9550]	1870-1899
Third series	[Cd.1]-[Cd.9239]	1900-1918
Fourth series	[Cmd.1]-Cmd.9889	1919-1956
Fifth series	Cmnd.1-	1956-date

The Bills and Papers, when bound in their sessional series, are arranged, not in numerical order, but in subject groups in the following manner:

1. *Public Bills,* alphabetically by title. This serves to bring together the various stages of a Bill, which bear different numbers depending on the date of introduction into the House.

2. *Reports from Committees,* alphabetically by subject or by the name of the Committee.

3. *Reports from Commissioners, Inspectors,* etc., alphabetically by subject.

4. *Accounts and Papers* (including all documents that do not fall under the other headings), by an order that may seem to be arbitrary but is invariable: Finance coming first, followed by papers relating to security and defence, the Civil Estimates, and finally Trade and Navigation Accounts and the State Papers.

5. *The Sessional Index,* listing the Bills, Papers, and Command Papers by number and then giving a detailed alphabetical index.

Since each volume in these sets comprises a number of separately paged documents, the sets preserved in the House of Commons are marked with continuous pagination for each volume, and the *Sessional Index* cites this pagination in referring to the documents. Few libraries, in binding their sets, go to the trouble of adding this pagination, so that the citations serve only as an approximate guide to the location of a document in a given volume. Some libraries aid their users considerably by marking the page reference on the title page of each document.

Citations to the Sessional Papers are generally given in abbreviated form, identifying the document as follows: House (H.L. for House of Lords, H.C. for House of Commons), sessional year, Paper number in parentheses or Command Paper number without parentheses (but in brackets to 1922), volume in roman numerals, page reference in arabic numerals. For example:

Historic Buildings Council for England. 10th annual report, 1962. H.C. 1962/63 (215), Vol. xix, p. 645.

Statistics of foreigners entering and leaving the United Kingdom, 1962. H.C. 1962/63 Cmnd.2008, Vol. xxvii, p.13.

Reference to the Sessional Papers is made most easily by means of the *General Indexes,* covering the Bills, Reports, and Papers from 1801 to 1958/59, and the *Sessional Indexes* from 1959/60 to the present. The *Catalogue of Government Publications* may also be used in order to determine whether publications are parliamentary, but it gives neither volume nor page references to the Sessional Papers. Also, since the *Catalogue* is based on the calendar year, the papers of a single session are usually divided between two annual indexes.

Indexes and Guides to British Government Publications

A brief survey of other available indexes and guides to British government publications may be of value. There are three principal sources of information: the *General Indexes,* the annual catalogues, and the unofficial guides.

General Indexes

Access to the contents of the parliamentary papers is provided chiefly by a series of sessional and cumulated indexes. There is a sessional index for the papers of each session since 1806/7. The earliest cumulated *General Index* is for the period 1801/26, and cumulated indexes cover varying periods until a regular decennial pattern of publication begins with the *General Index* of 1870-1878/79. The most important of the indexes are the fifty-year cumulated *General Indexes.* They have been used as a principal source of information for this bibliography, and the entries in the present work include references to the subject headings used in them. The *General Indexes* to date are:

General Index to the Accounts and Papers, Reports of Commissioners, Estimates, etc. etc. Printed by Order of the House of Commons, or Presented by Command: 1801-1852 . . . [London, 1853]

> *General Alphabetical Index to the Bills, Reports, Estimates, Accounts, and Papers, Printed by Order of the House of Commons, and to the Papers Presented by Command, 1852-1899.* Ordered, by the House of Commons, to be Printed, 27 September 1909. London, Printed for His Majesty's Stationery Office, by Eyre and Spottiswoode, Ltd. Printers to the King's Most Excellent Majesty. [1909]

> *General Index to the Bills, Reports and Papers Printed by Order of the House of Commons and to the Reports and Papers Presented by Command 1900 to 1948-49.* London, Her Majesty's Stationery Office, 1960.

These three major cumulations are supplemented by one decennial index for the period since 1950:

> *General Alphabetical Index to the Bills, Reports and Papers Printed by Order of the House of Commons and to the Reports and Papers Presented by Command 1950 to 1958-59.* London, Her Majesty's Stationery Office, 1963.

For most practical purposes the fifty-year cumulations supersede the decennial indexes. However, when working with the papers of a limited period, it is sometimes easier to use the decennial *General Index* for that period. The indexing method is somewhat simpler, and one does not have to scan the entries for half a century to find a desired reference.

The arrangement of material in the *General Indexes* is by subject, though the subject headings used in the three fifty-year cumulations are by no means uniform. The 1852-99 *General Index* makes the most frequent departures from the norm and also omits the Sessional or Command Paper number from its entries, so that one cannot obtain from it a complete and accurate citation. Despite this fault, it remains the most convenient tool for locating documents in the Sessional Papers of its period.

The subject headings in the *General Indexes* are subdivided according to the nature of the material, generally into four groups indicated by roman numerals: I, Bills; II, Reports from Committees; III, Reports from Commissioners; IV, Accounts and Papers. This arrangement corresponds to the sequence used in bound sets of the Sessional Papers, described earlier in this Introduction. Within each group, entries are numbered with arabic numerals, and the arrangement is generally alphabetical.

The *General Indexes* list all parliamentary serials, but they do not indicate changes from parliamentary to non-parliamentary publications; they simply stop short when parliamentary publication ceases. Nor do they show when a publication is superseded or continued by another. It is sometimes possible to ascertain from the *Sessional Indexes* that such a change has occurred, but the search is tedious. Since the listing in these parliamentary indexes is by subject, the agency responsible for issuing a paper is not indicated unless its name happens to appear in the title.

Annual Catalogues

An annual catalogue of government publications is issued by the Stationery Office. Begun in 1922 as the *Consolidated List of Government Publications* and now entitled *Catalogue of Government Publications,* it cumulates monthly catalogues arranged in the same manner and includes all government publications, both parliamentary and non-parliamentary. It lists separately the parliamentary publications—Sessional Papers, Bills, and Command Papers— by number, and non-parliamentary publications by agency. From 1936, it is paged continuously for five-year periods, with a cumulated index. The catalogue is much improved since 1949 by the listing of parliamentary papers under the appropriate agency heading in the non-parliamentary section as well as by number in the parliamentary section. Prior to 1922, separate catalogues of non-parliamentary publications were issued; but neither they nor the publications that they list are widely available.

Unofficial Guides

Taylor, Ruby Lane. *Guide to the Serial and Periodical Publications in Great Britain. Parliament. Sessional Papers. 1914-1933.* Preliminary edition (John Crerar Library Reference List no. 30). Chicago, 1934.

The present work gained its inspiration from Mrs. Taylor's *Guide* and follows the same general plan, though the scope has been much expanded.

Mrs. Taylor's work covered a period of rapid and confusing change in parliamentary publishing: many serials were suspended or discontinued during the First World War, and many of those that resumed publication changed from parliamentary to non-parliamentary status as a result of postwar economy campaigns. Such changes, found most frequently in the years 1920-22, can be a serious obstacle to scholars who wish to examine a complete set of the reports or accounts of a government agency. Not only might one assume from the indexes to parliamentary papers that many titles had ceased to exist, but for practical purposes they did cease to exist in many libraries, since they no longer arrived automatically as part of a subscription to the Sessional Papers.

When Mrs. Taylor completed her *Guide* in 1934, it probably seemed that a relatively stable situation had at last arrived. But within the decade another world war was to bring about a further drastic reduction in governmental publishing, while the social revolution that followed the war has more than compensated for the temporary decrease by producing a never ending proliferation of new agencies and legislation. The increase in titles is substantial: Mrs. Taylor recorded some 500 serials; the present work lists almost 1,300 entries.

A useful list of British government serials is found in:

List of the Serial Publications of Foreign Governments, 1815-1931; edited
by Winifred Gregory for the American Council of Learned Societies,
American Library Association, National Research Council . . . New York,
H. W. Wilson Company, 1932.

The listing in this work is by agency, and it records holdings in a number of
American libraries. No distinction is made between parliamentary and non-
parliamentary publications, and the cutoff date of 1931 now severely limits
its usefulness.

The sources listed above and the parliamentary papers themselves are the
principal authorities for the listing of titles in this bibliography. Examples of
each title have been examined; in all cases, the first and the last issue to
appear in the parliamentary papers have been inspected, as well as those
issued at dates when major changes in title or variations in the pattern of
issue occurred. The *Catalogue of Government Publications* has been used as
the principal guide to the existence of serials in non-parliamentary form.
Reference has also been made, when necessary, to the Library of Congress
Catalog, the British Museum *General Catalogue of Printed Books,* the
British National Bibliography, and the *British Union Catalogue of Periodicals.*

Variations in Listing British Government Agencies

There are wide variations in the manner of listing British government
agencies. In the present work I have preferred British practice to that of the
Library of Congress when they differ, and have given strongest weight to the
form used in the publications themselves. Mrs. Taylor followed the Library of
Congress *Catalog* and *Serial Publications of Foreign Governments* in listing
separately the publications issued by Irish and Scottish departments. In the
case of Ireland this practice is reasonable. The political union of Ireland with
Great Britain dated only from 1800, and Irish departments generally remained
quite distinct until the partition of Ireland in 1922 into the Irish Free State
and Northern Ireland. Each has its own parliament, and many publications
that formerly appeared in the British parliamentary papers have been continued in some form by their respective governments. Publications of Irish
departments are, therefore, listed separately at the end of the bibliography.
Scotland, however, is very different. The links with the government of the
United Kingdom are much closer, and although there are some departments
dealing specifically with Scottish affairs, many matters concerning both
Scotland and England are the direct responsibility of Ministries in London.
Also, changes in the administrative pattern are quite frequent. Consequently,
I have followed the usual British practice of listing Scottish departments in

their alphabetical position with other British departments.

The standard sources also differ considerably in their assignment of agency responsibility for many publications. They disagree most frequently when the Exchequer and Audit Department or the Treasury is involved. The accounts prepared by departments are generally audited by the Exchequer and Audit Department before being presented to Parliament together with a report by the Comptroller and Auditor General. It would thus be possible to list them either under the department which had prepared the accounts or under the Exchequer and Audit Department. I have preferred the former, since it gives a much better indication of the range of subjects with which each department is concerned.

Arrangement of Material in the Bibliography

The arrangement of material in the present bibliography is as follows. The agencies responsible for issuing publications are listed alphabetically, except for Irish departments, which are listed in a separate alphabetical sequence at the end. Title entries are given in alphabetical order under their agencies and are numbered consecutively. Occasionally a number may be omitted (as no. 77) when a title has been deleted in the revision of the manuscript; the addition of a letter (as "a") to an entry number signifies an entry added in the revision (no. 631a). The combined subject and agency index refers to entry numbers rather than to pages; it should be particularly useful in view of the fact that related material is often dispersed under several agencies.

Under each major agency heading, and under most of the current minor agencies, are given a brief summary of its origin, the principal changes in its responsibilities and title, and its relationship to other agencies. An asterisk before the names of agencies referred to in these notes indicates that the bibliography also contains entries under those agencies. Thus the user is given a general reference to related material which may otherwise be overlooked. For example, the Ministry of Transport, when established in 1919, assumed many functions that formerly belonged to the Board of Trade. Many of its publications are similar to titles issued earlier by the Board of Trade, even though not all are direct continuations. The asterisk alerts the user to this relationship between agencies. When the agency responsible for a continuous publication has changed, the title is entered under the latest agency responsible.

Each numbered entry in the bibliography may consist of up to four elements:

1. *Title, volume, and date.* Entries are based on the latest title used, and long titles are shortened when this will not cause confusion. Volume or serial numbers are given when available, though they are now used in very few series. The dates given are those of coverage rather than of publication. To give both is confusing, and the dates covered by a report

or account are the more important. The papers are almost invariably found in the session of the same year or the year following the date covered, with the exception of the Estimates, which, of course, appear in the year preceding the date covered. A plus symbol (+) denotes a serial which was ongoing at the time of compilation.

2. *Notes.* Immediately following the title, volume, and date is noted any useful information about the title: for example, a statement that it continues or supersedes another title, or that it is itself continued or superseded by another. Less direct relationship to earlier or later publications is also noted, as are significant changes in the issuing agency. Important title changes are listed; minor title changes, very frequent in government serials, are indicated simply by the note "Title varies."

3. *Parliamentary and non-parliamentary publication.* Unless otherwise noted, titles listed are to be found entirely in the Sessional Papers. But when any portion of a serial has been issued in non-parliamentary form, the dates of issue in both parliamentary papers and non-parliamentary form are shown, by the abbreviations PP and NP. Gaps in the publication of normally regular serials are also indicated.

4. *Reference to the General Indexes.* The final item in each entry, except in those commencing publication after 1959, is a reference to the subject headings used in the principal cumulated *General Indexes* to the parliamentary papers, listed earlier in this Introduction. Since many of the subject headings in the fifty-year cumulations are very lengthy, the numbered subdivision of the subject heading is given when necessary in order to facilitate reference. For some of the longer subject headings only the key words are given, provided that there is no possibility of confusion with any other heading. When the period covered by a title spans more than one *General Index,* references to the subject headings in them are separated by semicolons; however, the subject heading itself is not repeated unless a change in subject heading is to be noted. Some examples may clarify this point:

Entry no. 4: Yeomanry cavalry training return . . . 1879-1908.

Yeomanry

The dates of coverage indicate that the title will appear both in the 1852-99 *General Index* and in the 1900-1948/49 *General Index.* The single subject-heading reference *Yeomanry* shows that the same heading is used in both *Indexes.* Unlike the example that follows, notation of subdivisions is not necessary for easy location of the entry.

Entry no. 12: Naval prize money, bounty, salvage, etc. Account . . .
1854/55-1906/7.

Prize money; Navy V.41

This entry also appears in two *General Indexes,* but a different
subject heading is used in the later *Index.* Moreover, the heading for
Navy is complicated, so a precise reference is given to the subdivision at which this serial will be found.

Entry no. 53: Divisional reports . . . by the Inspectors of Schools . . .
1886-1902.

Education and schools III.6; III.15

Again, the entry appears in two *Indexes.* Since the subject heading
remains the same in both, it is not repeated. But the headings are
long enough to make a precise reference to each *Index* desirable, and
a semicolon separates the two references.

Time Limitation

Publications that ceased before 1900 are excluded from this bibliography.
Consideration was given to including them, but to do so would greatly have
increased the bulk of the volume, with very little advantage. Many nineteenth-
century titles are no longer of great significance and they are easily traced,
since almost all government serials of this period appear in the parliamentary
papers. One may readily identify and locate them in *Serial Publications of
Foreign Governments* or the *General Indexes* to the parliamentary papers.

Abbreviations
and Symbols

NP	Non-parliamentary papers
n.s.	New series
PP	Parliamentary papers
S.I.	Statutory instrument
*	Used in notes under agency headings to indicate that entries also appear under other related agencies so marked
+	Ongoing publication at the time of compilation

Note: The final item in italic in each entry, except in those commencing publication after 1959, is a reference to the subject headings used in the principal cumulated *General Indexes* to the parliamentary papers.

Great Britain

excluding Ireland

Aberdeen. University

1
Annual report on the state of the finances . . . 1889/90-1913/14.
　Title varies: Abstract of accounts . . .
　　Universities and colleges (Scotland)

2
Annual statistical report . . . 1898/99-1913/14.
　　Universities and colleges (Scotland)

Adjutant General's Office

Adjutants General existed as long ago as the middle of the seventeenth century, and the office became important in the late eighteenth century. In 1895 it became a separate department and one of the principal divisions of the *War Office.

3
Militia units. Return showing the establishment of each unit of militia in the United Kingdom . . . 1859/62-1907.
　　Militia

4
Yeomanry cavalry training return . . . 1879-1908.
　　Yeomanry

Admiralty

One of the most ancient departments. Admirals with local functions existed in the thirteenth century, and the office of Lord High Admiral was put into commission in 1547. The present structure dates from the Admiralty Act of 1690, which vested powers in a Board of Commissioners. The Defence (Transfer of Functions) Act 1964 consolidated administration of the three fighting Services under the *Ministry of Defence.

5
Battle practice. Result . . . 1905-1913.
　　Navy V.7

6
Casualties to ships on the Navy list. Return . . . 1901-1906.
　　Navy V.11

---

*The asterisk indicates a reference to another government agency, listed in this bibliography, issuing similar or related publications.

7
Courts-martial. Returns of the number of courts-martial held and summary

punishment inflicted on seamen of the Royal Navy. 1874-1912.
Courts martial; Navy V.13

8
Fleets (the British Commonwealth of nations and foreign countries). Particulars of the fleets . . . 1886-1939.
Navy and marines VI.72 (xxv); Navy V.23

9
Gunnery. Result of test of gunlayers in His Majesty's Fleet . . . 1903-1914.
Title varies: Results of the prize firing . . .; Results of gunlayers' competitions . . .
Navy V.27

10
Naval expenditure (principal naval powers). Return . . . 1880/1903-1905/15.
Navy V.19

11
Naval manoeuvres. Report . . . 1887-1906.
Title varies.
Navy and marines IV.22; VI.42; Navy III.8

12
Naval prize money, bounty, salvage, etc. Account . . . 1854/55-1906/7.
Prize money; Navy V.41

13
Naval savings banks. An account of deposits, payments and of interest . . . 1866/67-1919/20.
Savings banks

14
Naval works. Expenditure to date, etc. Statement showing total estimated cost of each naval work . . . 1897/98-1907/9.
Navy and marines VI.83; Navy V.65

15
Naval Works Act 1905. Memorandum showing progress and expenditure, etc. on items included in the Naval Works Act. 1905-1908.
Navy V.65

16
Naval Works Acts. Account . . . 1898/99-1908/9.
Navy V.65

17
Navy estimates . . . 1810-1963/64.
From 1964/65 incorporated in: Ministry of Defence. Defence estimates.
Navy and marines V.1; Navy IV.1

18
Navy estimates. Statement of the First Lord of the Admiralty explanatory of the Navy estimates . . . 1887/88-1962/63.
From 1963 incorporated in: Ministry of Defence. Statement on the Defence estimates.
Not issued: 1915/16-1918/19, 1940/41-1946/47.
Navy and marines V.2; Navy IV.8

19
Navy estimates. Supplementary estimates . . . 1834/35-1962/63.
Later under: Ministry of Defence. Navy Department.
Navy and marines V.4; Navy IV.10

20
Navy estimates (shipbuilding programme). Statement showing the probable effect . . . 1902/3-1925/26.
Title varies: Shipbuilding programme (effect of estimates, etc.). Statement . . .
Not issued: 1914/15-1919/20, 1921/22-1924/25.
Navy IV.6

21
Navy (victualling yards manufacturing accounts). Annual balance sheets at the Home Yards and Malta Yards . . . 1862/63-1913/14.
Title varies: to 1888, Balance sheet of cost of manufacturing and repairing articles on conversion.
Malta Yards not included until 1891/92.
Dockyards

22
Peterhead Harbour. Reports respecting . . . works. 1888-1913/14.
Peterhead Harbour

23
Statement of excess. Navy. Statement of the sum required to be voted to make good excesses of Navy expenditure . . . 1841/42-1956/57.
Title varies: Navy estimates. Statement of excess . . .

Irregular.
> *Navy III.13; Navy and marines V.7;*
> *Navy IV.3*

Admiralty. Medical Department of the Navy

24
Statistical report on the health of the Navy. 1830/36-1936.
> Early issues irregular.
> PP: 1830/36-1914.
> NP: 1915-1936.
> Not Issued: 1916-1920
> *Navy III.5; Statistical tables II.3;*
> *Navy III.5*

Advisory Council on Scientific Policy

The Council was appointed in January 1947 and was superseded in 1964 by the *Council for Scientific Policy.

25
Annual report . . . 1-7, 1947/48-1963/64.
> *Scientific policy*

Aeronautical Research Committee

The Committee superseded the *Aeronautics Advisory Committee.

26
Report. 1920/21-1932/33.
> PP: 1, 1920/21.
> NP: 1921/22-1932/33.
> *Air III.22*

Aeronautics Advisory Committee

The Committee was superseded by the *Aeronautical Research Committee.

27
Report. 1909/10-1919/20.
> *Air III.2*

Agricultural, Horticultural and Forestry Industry Training Board

Established August 1966 under Industrial Training Act 1964.

28
Report and statement of accounts . . . 1966/67 +.

Agricultural Land Commission

Established October 1947 under Agriculture Act 1947, to manage and farm land vested in the Minister, and to advise and assist in matters relating to the management of agricultural land. The Commission was dissolved in 1963, its powers becoming a direct responsibility of the *Ministry of Agriculture, Fisheries and Food.

29
Report . . . 1-17, 1948-1963.
> *Agriculture*

Agricultural Research Council

Incorporated by Royal Charter, July 1930. In April 1956 assumed responsibility under the Agricultural Research Act for grant-aiding and administration of independent agricultural research institutes.

30
Accounts . . . 1931/32-1941/42.
> *Agriculture IV.20*

31
Report . . . 1-3, 1930/33-1935/37; 1956/57+.
> *Agriculture III.6*

Air Ministry

Established January 1918, replacing the Air Board which had been set up in 1916. The Defence (Transfer of Functions) Act 1964 consolidated administration of the three fighting Services under the *Ministry of Defence.

32

Air estimates . . . 1918/19-1963/64.
From 1964/65 incorporated in: Ministry of Defence. Defence estimates.
Air IV.1; Air Force III

33

Air estimates. Memorandum by the Secretary of State for Air to accompany Air estimates . . . 1919/20-1962/63.
Title varies: Air estimates. Statement . . .
From 1963 incorporated in: Ministry of Defence. Statement on the Defence estimates.
Not issued: 1939/40-1945/46.
Air IV.4; Air Force III

34

Air services. Supplementary estimate. Estimate of the further sum required to be voted . . . 1920/21-1962/63.
Later supplementary estimates issued by: Ministry of Defence. Air Force Department.
Air IV.5; Air Force III

Air Ministry. Directorate of Civil Aviation

35

Annual report on the progress of civil aviation . . . 1919-1938.
Half-yearly to March 1922. First report titled: Synopsis of progress of work in the Department of Civil Aviation . . .
Note also later NP: Ministry of Civil Aviation. Civil aviation report . . . 1946/47-1948/49.
PP: 1919-1926.
NP: 1927-1938.
Air III.11

Air Transport Advisory Council

The Council was established under the Civil Aviation Act 1946 and was superseded by the *Air Transport Licensing Board.

36

Report . . . and statement by the Minister . . . 1-13, 1947/48-1960/61.
Air III.25; Aviation, civil II

Air Transport Licensing Board

Established under the Civil Aviation (Licensing) Act 1960, superseding the *Air Transport Advisory Council.

37

Report. 1, 1960/61+.

Ancient Monuments Boards for England, Scotland and Wales

Established 1953 under the Ancient Monuments Consolidation and Amendment Act 1913, as extended by Section 16 of the Historic Buildings and Ancient Monuments Act 1953.

38

Annual reports . . . 1, 1954+.
Historic buildings and ancient monuments

Bank of England

Founded in 1694, the Bank took over the circulation of exchequer bills in the early eighteenth century. It has been receiving revenue and making government payments since the beginning of the nineteenth century.

39

Annual accounts of exchequer bills and other government securities . . . 1836-1925/26.
Bank of England

40

Report . . . 1946/47+.
Presented pursuant to Bank of England Act 1946.
PP: 1946/47-1958/59.
NP: 1959/60+.
Bank of England

Board of Agriculture and Fisheries

Established in 1889 as the Board of Agriculture, taking over powers and duties of the Privy Council Agricultural Department and the Land Commission. Title changed 1903, when responsibility for fisheries (with the exception of deepsea fisheries) was transferred from the *Board of Trade. In December 1919 the Board was renamed the *Ministry of Agriculture and Fisheries.

41
Annual report of the Education Branch on the distribution of grants for agricultural education. 1888/89-1914/15.
Title varies. Only 1913/14-1914/15 shown as Education Branch.
Agriculture IV.7; III.13, III.6

42
Annual report on the administration of the grant for the encouragement and improvement of the light horse-breeding industry . . . 1911/12-1913/14.
Horses

43
Annual report on the administration of the grant for the encouragement and improvement of the livestock breeding industry . . . 1914/15.
Cattle and livestock

44
Crown Lands Act 1906. Report by the President of the Board of Agriculture and Fisheries, as a Commissioner of Woods, Forests, and Land Revenues . . . 1-3, 1907-1909.
3rd Report not issued separately, but included in Crown Estate Commissioners' 87th Report.
Woods, forests, etc.

45
Development and Road Improvement Funds Act 1909. Memorandum showing advances from the Development Fund . . . 1911/12-1912/13.
Development and Road Improvement Fund

46
Joint annual report of the Forestry Branches of the Board of Agriculture and the Office of Woods and Forests . . . 1, 1912/13.
Later, see: Forestry Commission. Annual report . . . 1919/20+.
Forestry

Board of Agriculture and Fisheries. Commercial Control Branch

47
Annual report . . . Proceedings under the Sale of Food and Drugs Acts . . . 1913-1914.
Continues: Board of Agriculture and Fisheries. Intelligence Division. Annual report . . .
Agriculture III.7

Board of Agriculture and Fisheries. Horticulture Branch

48
Annual report . . . Proceedings under the Destructive Insects and Pests Acts . . . 1912/13-1913/14.
Continues: Board of Agriculture and Fisheries. Intelligence Division. Annual report . . .
Continued by: Ministry of Agriculture and Fisheries. Intelligence Department. Report . . . 1921/24-1924/26 (NP).
Agriculture III.7

Board of Agriculture and Fisheries. Intelligence Division

49
Annual report of proceedings . . . 1900-1912.
From 1907 issued in two parts:
Pt. I. Proceedings under the Sale of Food and Drugs Acts . . . 1907-1912. (Continued as: Board of Agriculture and Fisheries. Commercial Control Branch. Annual report . . .)
Pt. II. Proceedings under the Destructive Insects and Pests Acts . . . 1907-1911/12. (Continued as: Board of Agriculture and Fisheries. Horticulture Branch. Annual report . . .)
Agriculture III.7

Board of Control

Established by the Mental Deficiency
Act 1913, taking over powers of the
*Lunacy Commission. It was dissolved
in November 1960 under the Mental
Health Act 1959, its functions being
taken over by the *Ministry of Health
and by Mental Health Review Tribunals.

50
Lunacy and Mental Treatment Acts.
Annual report of the Board of Control
... 1-47, 1914-1959.
    Title varies: Lunacy and mental de-
ficiency ...
    Continues: Lunacy Commission. Luna-
cy. Copy of the ... report ...
    From 1960, information on mental
health is included in: Ministry of Health.
On the state of the public health ...
    PP: 1, Pt. I, 1914; 2-7, 1915-1920;
23-47, 1937/38-1959.
    NP: 1, Pt. II, 1914; 8-23, 1921-
1936.
    Not issued: 26-31, 1939/40-1944/45.
                Lunacy; Mental health

Board of Education

Established by the Board of Education
Act 1899, replacing the Education De-
partment and the Department of Science
and Art; its responsibilities included
administration of museums and libraries.
The Education Act 1944 abolished the
Board and established the *Ministry of
Education.

51
Code of regulations: day and elementary
schools ... 1860-1920.
    Title varies.
        Education and schools IV.6; IV.5

52
Code of regulations: evening and technical schools ... 1892-1918.
    Title varies.
        Education and schools IV.10; IV.6

53
Divisional reports ... by the Inspectors
of Schools ... 1886-1902.
        Education and schools III.6; III.15

54
Elementary education. Statistics relating
to receipts and expenditure of local
education authorities. 1911/12-1918/19.
        Education and schools IV.24

55
General reports of H.M. Inspectors on
science and art schools and classes and
evening schools, and of examiners in
science and art. 1901.
        Education and schools III.32

56
General reports on higher education,
with appendices. 1902.
        Education and schools III.14

57
Grants, accounts, and loans. Statement
showing (1) Schools in receipt of parliamentary grants; (2) Grants paid to
school boards ... ; (3) School board
accounts and list of loans. 1895/96-
1903/4.
    Title varies.
        Education and schools IV.9(r); IV.37

58
Higher education (application of funds
by local authorities). Return ... 1892/
93-1906/7.
    Title varies: 1892/93-1902/3, Tech-
nical education ...
    Preceded by its: Technical education
(funds). Abstract of return ... 1890/93.
        Education and schools IV.28; IV.97

59
List of certified schools for the blind,
deaf, defective, and epileptic children in
England and Wales ... 1906-1939.
    PP: 1906-1918.
    NP: 1920-1939.
    Not issued: 1915-1917.
        Education and schools IV.4

60
List of evening schools under the administration of the Board ... 1903/4-
1905/6.
        Education and schools IV.33

61
List of school boards and school attendance committees in England and Wales
... 1880-1902.
        Education and schools IV.25; IV.67

62
List of schools under the administration of the Board . . . 1901/2-1903/4.
Education and schools IV.11

63
Medical treatment (grants). Regulations under which grants in respect of medical treatment and care of children . . . will be made . . . 1912/13-1917.
Education and schools IV.48

64
Monthly statement of schemes for the formation of education committees . . . March 1903-Aug./Nov. 1903.
Education and schools IV.21

65
Public elementary schools warned. Quarterly returns . . . 1894-1903.
Education and schools IV.9(2c); IV.25

66
Regulations for secondary day schools . . . 1902/3-1909/10; 1917/18; 1921.
Education and schools IV.77

67
Regulations for the preliminary education of elementary school teachers . . . 1904/5-1909.
Title varies.
Education and schools IV.56

68
Regulations for the training of teachers . . . 1904-1919.
Education and schools IV.93

69
Regulations for the training of teachers of domestic subjects . . . 1907-1909/10.
Education and schools IV.93

70
Regulations providing for special grants-in-aid of certain local education authorities in England and Wales . . . 1906-1918/19.
PP: 1906-1916/17, 1918/19.
NP: 1917/18.
Education and schools IV.40

71
Report of the Board of Education. 1899/1900-1938.
Continues Reports of the Education

Department and the Department of Science and Art.
Continued by: Ministry of Education. Education in . . . Report of the Ministry of Education . . . 1947-1963.
Education and schools III.1

72
Report on schools for the blind and deaf. 1896/97-1898/1900.
Blind and deaf mutes III.4; Education and schools III.5

73
Report on the Science Museum, and on the Geological Survey and the Museum of Practical Geology . . . 1908-1919.
Continues in part: Board of Education. Report . . . on the Victoria and Albert Museum, the Royal College of Science and of Art, etc. . . .
Continued in two separate publications (NP): Geological Survey. Summary of progress of the Geological Survey . . . ; and: Board of Education. Science Museum. Annual report of the Advisory Council . . .
Museums; etc.

74
Report . . . on the Victoria and Albert Museum, the Royal College of Science and of Art, the Geological Survey and Museum, and on the work of the Solar Physics Committee. 1901-1907.
Title varies: 1901-1902, Museums, colleges, and institutions under the administration of the Board. Report . . .
Continued by two publications: Victoria and Albert Museum. Review . . . (Report, 1908-1918); and: Report on the Science Museum . . .
Museums, etc.

75
Reports from universities and university colleges participating in the parliamentary grant . . . 1894-1913/14.
Continued by: University Grants Committee. Report.
Two series of reports were published for 1906/7, when all the reports were, for the first time, made to relate to the same academic year.
Universities and colleges III.5; III.3

76
Reports on training colleges . . . 1886-

1900.
Education and schools III.22; III.41

78
Science and art (regulations). Regulations relating to museums and institutions . . . 1902/3-1906/7.
Museums, etc.

79
Special reports on education subjects. 1-28, 1896/97-1914.
PP: 1-23, 1896/97-1909.
NP: 24-28, 1911-1914.
Education and schools III.1; III.34

80
Statement of grants available from the Board of Education in aid of technological and professional work in universities in England and Wales. 1911-1915.
Universities and colleges IV.8

81
Statistics of public education in England and Wales. 1899/1900-1925/26.
Title varies: 1899/1900-1905/7, Statistics of public elementary day schools.
From 1906-1913/14 published in two parts: Pt. 1, Educational statistics; Pt. 2, Financial statistics.
PP: 1899/1900-1913/14, Pt. 1.
NP: 1919/20-1925/26.
Not issued: 1913/14 Pt. 2, 1914/15-1918/19.
Education and schools IV.84

82
Victoria and Albert Museum. Review of the principal acquisitions (with which is incorporated, as an appendix, the Annual report on the Museum). 1908-1938.
Title and contents vary: 1908-1919, Report on the Victoria and Albert Museum . . .;1908, includes report on the Royal College of Art; 1908-1919, includes report on the Bethnal Green Museum.
Continues in part: Board of Education. Report . . . on the Victoria and Albert Museum, the Royal College of Science and of Art, etc. . . . .
PP: 1908-1917.
NP: 1918-1938.
Victoria and Albert Museum

83
Voluntary schools (associated and un-associated schools). Shares of grant, etc. Return . . . 1897/98-1903/5.
Title varies: Grants, accounts and loans. Return . . .
Education and schools IV.31; IV.100

Board of Education. Welsh Department

84
Education in Wales. Report of the Board of Education under the Welsh Intermediate Education Act 1889. 1893/94-1938.
1893/94-1899 issued by Charity Commissioners.
Education and schools III.9; III.16

85
Education in Wales. Statistics of public education . . . 1912/13-1925/26.
PP: 1912/13-1913/14, Pt. I.
NP: 1919/20-1925/26.
Not issued: 1913/14, Pt. II: 1914/15-1918/19; 1922/23-1923/24.
Education and schools IV.84

86
Regulations for secondary schools in Wales . . . 1907/8-1909/10; 1917/18; 1921.
Education and schools IV.77

Board of Manufactures in Scotland

87
National Gallery, etc. Annual report as to their proceedings . . . 1-13, 1893/94-1905/6.
Continued by: Board of Trustees for the National Galleries of Scotland. Report.
National Gallery, etc. (Scotland)

Board of Trade

The oldest executive committee of the Privy Council, established by an Order in Council of 1786 which dissolved several earlier bodies dating to 1622. Responsibilities have varied widely: fisheries were transferred to the *Board of

Agriculture and Fisheries in 1903; railways, canals, and other transportation matters to the *Ministry of Transport in 1919.

88
Abstract of foreign labour statistics . . . 1-4, 1898/99-1910.
Statistical tables III.13; Labour IV.13

89
Alcoholic beverages. Statement showing the production and consumption . . . in . . . Europe, in the United States and in the principal British colonies . . . 1885/-96-1895/1909.
1885/96 covers only Europe and United States; colonies added in 1885/97.
Alcoholic beverages; Alcohol

90
Alien immigration (from the Continent of Europe). Return of the number of aliens that arrived from the Continent at ports in the United Kingdom in each month . . . 1891-1905.
Continued by: Home Office. Aliens Act 1905. Return . . .
Emigration and immigration IV.4; Aliens IV.2

91
Annual statement of the navigation and shipping of the United Kingdom . . . 1871-1938.
Statement for 1917 gives comparative tables for 1913-1917.
PP: 1871-1920.
NP: 1921-1938.
Not issued: 1914-1916.
Trade IV.8; IV.41

92
Assurance companies' returns. Statements of assurance business . . . 1911-1958.
Presented pursuant to Assurance Companies Act 1909.
Pt. A continues its: Life assurance companies. Statements of accounts . . .
PP: 1911-1918.
NP: 1919-1958.
Assurance IV.1

93
Bankruptcy. General annual report . . .

1883+.
Single report issued for years 1939/53.
PP: 1883-1920.
NP: 1921+.
Bankruptcy III

94
Bankruptcy and companies (winding-up) proceedings. Account . . . 1870+.
Title varies: 1891/92-1914/15, Companies (Winding-up) Act 1890. Account . . .
Accounts for 1915/16-1920/21 included in its: Bankruptcy. General annual report . . .
Not issued: 1915/16-1925/26; 1940/41-1954/55.
Bankruptcy IV.22; Companies IV.7; Bankruptcy IV

95
Boiler explosions. Report by the Board of Trade upon the working of the Boiler Explosions Acts, with appendices. 1882/83+.
Issued by the Ministry of Transport, 1946-1961.
PP: 1882/83-1916/17.
NP: 1917/18+.
Not issued: 1939-1945.
Boilers

96
British Shipping (Assistance) Acts 1935 and 1936. Statement of the distribution of the tramp shipping subsidy . . . 1935-1936.
Shipping

97
British shipping (continuance of subsidy). Memorandum on the financial resolution . . . 1934/35-1936/37.
Shipping

98
Capital, traffic, receipts, etc. General report to the Board of Trade in regard to the share and loan capital, traffic in passengers and goods, etc. . . . of the railway companies of the United Kingdom . . . 1871-1901.
Railways IV.10; IV.4

99
Census of production. 1-5, 1907-1935; 1948+.

PP: 1, 1907.
NP: 3-5, 1924-1935; 1948+.
Not issued: 2, 1912.

Production

100
Cinematograph Film Production (Special Loans) Acts 1949-1966. Account . . . 1949/50-1967/68.
Future accounts to be included in Civil appropriation accounts.

Cinematographs

101
Clothing Industry Development Council (Dissolution). Account of the sums recovered under Article 9 of the Clothing Industry Development Council (Dissolution) Order (S.I. 1952 No. 2238) and of their disposal . . . 1952/53-1967/68.

Clothing

102
Coal shipments. Tables giving details as to shipments of coal abroad . . . for each quarter . . . 1895/96-1914/15.
Title varies.

Coal IV.10

103
Colonial import duties. Return relating to the rates of import duties levied upon the principal and other articles imported into the British colonies, possessions, and protectorates . . . 1901-1915.

Colonies III.21

104
Commercial intelligence. Return showing the number of annual and other reports received . . . 1910-1913.

Trade IV.17

105
Commercial reports. 1880-1920.
Numbered serially each year, average 30 to 45 per annum in the 19th century, only about 5 per annum after 1900.
See also: Foreign Office. Diplomatic and consular reports . . .
1880-1899, see Appendix, p. 1549
of 1852/99 Index;
1900-1920, Trade III.10

106
The Commonwealth and the sterling area. Statistical abstract. 1-88, 1850/63-1967.

Title varies: Statistical abstract for the several British overseas dominions and protectorates . . . ; Statistical abstract for the British Empire . . . ; Statistical abstract for the British Commonwealth . . .
Not the same publication as its; Statistical abstract for the British Empire . . . 1889/1903-1899/1913.
PP: 1-70, 1850/63-1945/47.
NP: 71-88, 1947/50-1967.

Statistical tables III.2; Colonies III.35

107
Companies. General annual report. 1, 1890/91+.
PP: 1-30, 1890/91-1920.
NP: 31-48, 1920/21-1938; 1939/45+.

`Companies

108
Control of Office and Industrial Development Act 1965. Annual report by the Board of Trade. 1, 1965/66+.

109
Cooperative societies. Report on industrial and agricultural cooperative societies in the United Kingdom, with statistical tables. 1-2, 1901-1912.
1, 1901 as Report on workmen's cooperative societies . . .

Cooperative societies

110
Cotton (Centralised Buying) Act 1947. Account . . . 1947/48-1966/68.
Issued by Ministry of Materials, 1951/52-1953/54.

Cotton

111
Customs Duties (Dumping and Subsidies) Act 1957. Annual report by the Board of Trade . . . 1957/58+.

Customs and excise

112
Development of Inventions Acts 1948 to 1965. Account of the sums issued out of and received from the Consolidated Fund and of the sums received from the National Research Development Corporation . . . 1949/50-1965/66.

National Research Development
Corporation

113
Diplomatic reports (coal). Extracts relating to coal from the Reports received up to the present date from H. M. Diplomatic and Consular Officers abroad . . . 1902-1905.
Coal industry III.9

114
Distribution of German Enemy Property Acts 1949 and 1952. Account . . . 1951/53+.
Germany III

115
Electric Lighting Acts 1882+. Report respecting applications to, and proceedings of the Board of Trade . . . 1883-1914.
Continued by: Ministry of Transport. Electricity (Supply) Acts 1882 to 1928. Report . . .
Electric lighting; Electricity

116
Emigration and immigration . . . Copy of statistical tables relating to emigration and immigration from and into the United Kingdom . . . and report to the Board of Trade thereon . . . 1876-1913.
Statistical tables III.6; Emigration III.4

117
Employers' liability insurance companies. Statements deposited with the Board of Trade in pursuance of the Employers' Liability Insurance Companies Act 1907 . . . 1909-1910.
Workmen's compensation IV.4

118
Foreign trade and commerce . . . Accounts relating to the trade and commerce of certain foreign countries and British possessions. 1900-1939.
PP: 1900-1922.
NP: 1923-1939.
Trade IV.8

119
Gas and water orders . . . Report of the Board of Trade of their proceedings under the Gas and Water Works Facilities Act 1870 . . . 1900-1920.
Not issued: 1908, 1916-1919.
Gas and water III.4

120
Gas and Water Orders Confirmation Bill. Copy of memorandum stating the nature of the proposals contained in the Provisional Orders included in the Gas and Water Orders Provisional Bill. 1884-1904.
Gas, etc. IV.9; Gas and water IV.5

121
Gas and Water Works Facilities Act 1870. Special reports by the Board of Trade . . . 1890-1915.
Gas, etc. III.9; Gas and water III.12

122
Gas companies (metropolis). Accounts of the metropolitan gas companies . . . 1861-1906.
Gas, etc. IV.1; London IV.7

123
Gas undertakings . . . Return relating to all authorised gas undertakings in the United Kingdom other than those of local authorities . . . 1880-1920.
Continued in its: Gas undertakings. Return relating to all authorised gas undertakings in Great Britain. 1921-1947 (NP).
PP: 1880-1919.
NP: 1920.
Not issued: 1914-1918.
Gas, etc. IV.7; Gas and water IV.3

124
Gas undertakings (local authorities) . . . Return relating to all authorised gas undertakings in the United Kingdom . . . 1881/82-1920/21.
Continued in its: Gas undertakings. Return relating to all authorised gas undertakings in Great Britain. 1921-1947 (NP).
PP: 1881/82-1919/20.
NP: 1920/21.
Not issued: 1914/15-1918/19.
Gas, etc. IV.6; Gas and water IV.2

125
General Lighthouse Fund. Accounts . . . 1879/80+.
Issued by Ministry of Transport, 1947/48-1963/64.
Not issued: 1939/40-1944/45.
Lighthouses

126
Import duties. Statement of the rates of foreign import duties . . . 1901-1913.
Trade IV.27

127
Import Duties Act 1958. Annual report by the Board of Trade . . . 1, 1959/60+.

128
Imports and exports at prices of 1900. Tables . . . 1900/5-1900/13.
Trade IV.36

129
Investment grants. Annual report by the Board of Trade under the Industrial Development Act 1966 . . . 1, 1966/67+.

130
Iron and steel. Memorandum and statistical tables showing the production and consumption of iron ore and pig iron . . . 1890/1901-1908/12.
Title varies.
Iron and steel

131
Japanese Treaty of Peace Act 1951. Account . . . 1952/53+.
Japan

132
Life assurance companies. Statements of accounts . . . 1856-1910.
Continued by its: Assurance companies' returns . . . Pt. A.
Life assurance II.2; Assurance IV.1

133
Lighthouses, etc. (local inspection). Report to the Board of Trade by the Trinity House . . . of their inspection of local lighthouses . . . 1863-1911.
Lighthouses

134
Local Employment Acts 1960 to 1966. Accounts . . . 1960/61+.

135
Local Employment Acts 1960 to 1966. Annual report . . . 1, 1960/61+.

136
Loss of life at sea. Return . . . 1871/82-1893/1912.
Wrecks IV.11; II.4

137
Mercantile marine—examination for certificates of competency. Report on the examination of candidates for certificates of competency, and on sight tests . . . 1914-1920.
Merchant shipping III.3

138
Mercantile marine. Issue of certificates of competency. Return . . . 1911-1914.
Merchant shipping IV.5

139
Merchandise Marks Act 1926. Report of the Standing Committee . . . 1927+.
Reports irregular, each being on a specific product.
Merchandise marks; Patents

140
Merchant Seamen's Fund. Account of the receipt and expenditure under the Seamen's Fund Winding-up Act. 1852-1920.
Originally Mercantile Marine Fund. Not issued: 1915-1918.
Merchant shipping IV.10; IV.19

141
Merchant Shipping Acts 1876, 1894, 1906. Return of all British and foreign ships ordered by the Board of Trade . . . to be provisionally detained as unsafe. 1876-1914/15.
Merchant shipping IV.61; IV.12

142
Merchant Shipping Acts 1894 to 1938 (Dispensing Powers). Report by the Board of Trade of the cases in which they have exercised their powers under the Act . . . 1907/8-1938.
Merchant shipping III.9

143
Merchant shipping (loss of life). Return of the deaths of seamen and fishermen . . . 1908/9-1913/14.
Merchant shipping IV.9

144
Mining Industry Act 1926. Report by the Board of Trade on the working of Part I of the Act (Reorganisation of the Industry). 1-11, 1928-1938.
Mines III.13

145
Monopolies and Mergers Acts 1948 and 1965. Annual report . . . 1949+.
Title varies: until 1964, Monopolies and Restrictive Practices Acts . . .
Monopolies

146
Naval expenditure and mercantile marine (Great Britain, etc). Return . . . 1896-1904.
Navy V.22

147
Output of coal in the United Kingdom. Return showing the estimated quantities of coal raised in the United Kingdom in each of the quarters . . . 1915-1916.
Coal industry IV.19(d)

148
Passengers to and from places out of Europe (monthly). Return . . . June 1905-Dec. 1915.
Emigration

149
Pier and Harbour Provisional Orders Confirmation Memoranda. Memoranda stating the nature of the proposals contained in the Provisional Orders included in the Pier and Harbour Orders Confirmation Bills . . . 1884-1904.
Harbours

150
Piers and Harbours (Provisional Orders). Report by the Board of Trade of their proceedings under the General Pier and Harbour Act 1861 . . . 1862-1907.
Harbours

151
Pilotage. Abstract returns relating to pilotage in the United Kingdom . . . 1854/55-1938.
1913 not printed; 1913/18 covered by single Return.
Pilotage

152
Prices of exported coal. Return giving the quantities of coal exported from each of the principal ports in the United Kingdom in every quarterly period since the imposition of the coal duty in 1901

. . . 1905-1913.
Issued by Treasury, 1905-1909.
Coal industry IV.10

153
Railway accidents. Return of accidents and casualties, as reported to the Board of Trade by the railway companies in the United Kingdom . . . 1908-1915.
Annual. See also: Ministry of Transport. Railway accidents. Returns . . . (quarterly to 1920, then annual).
Railways IV.1(b)

154
Railway and Canal Traffic Act 1888. Report by the Board of Trade of proceedings under section 31 . . . including proceedings upon complaints . . . 1-13, 1889/90-1914.
Railways III.16; III.15

155
Railway companies (charitable and other contributions). Return showing in detail the amounts contributed by the railway companies . . . to institutions and associations not directly controlled by the companies, and not for the exclusive benefit of the companies' servants. 1907-1910.
Railways IV.6

156
Railway Companies Powers Act 1864. Report . . . on applications . . . and the proceedings of the Board of Trade with respect thereto. 1865-1914.
1865-1877 includes Railways Construction Facilities Act 1864. Report . . . (issued separately, 1878-1904).
Railways III.4; III.16

157
Railway, etc., Bills. Report by the Board of Trade upon all the bills and provisional orders . . . relating to railways, canals, tramways, harbours, and tidal waters, and the supply of electricity, gas and water . . . 1854-1914/16.
Title varies.
Bills, private

158
Railway returns. General report . . . in regard to the share and loan capital, traffic in passengers and goods, and the

working expenditure and net profits from railway working of the railway companies of the United Kingdom. 1871-1901.

Railways IV.10; IV.4

159
Railway Returns (Continuous Brakes) Act 1878. Return . . . by the railway companies of the United Kingdom . . . 1878-1903.

Railways IV.8; IV.2

160
Railway servants (hours of labour). Report . . . respecting proceedings under Railway Regulation Act 1893 . . . 1-22, 1893/94-1914/15.

Railways III.8; III.10

161
Railway servants (hours of labour). Return in pursuance of the Regulation of Railways Act 1889 of railway servants . . . July 1886-March 1914.

Railways IV.20(g); IV.16

162
Railways Construction Facilities Act 1864. Report by the Board of Trade on applications . . . and proceedings under that Act and Railways Powers and Construction Acts 1864. 1878-1904.

1865-1877, Report included in its: Railway Companies Powers Act 1864. Report . . .

Railways III.4; III.16

163
Ramsgate Harbour. Statement of the receipts and payments made by the Board of Trade . . . 1816-1906/7.

1816-1861 as Royal Harbour of Ramsgate Trust.

Ramsgate Harbour

164
Report on strikes and lock-outs in the United Kingdom . . . and on Conciliation and Arbitration Boards. 1888-1913.

Title varies.

Strikes and lock-outs; Trade boards III.8

165
Report on the life-saving apparatus on the coasts of the United Kingdom . . . 1902/3-1927.

Title varies: Rocket life-saving apparatus . . .

PP: 1910/11-1916/20.

NP: 1902/3-1909/10, 1920/21-1927.

Rockets

166
Sea Fisheries Act 1868. Orders for fishery grants. Report by the Board of Trade of their proceedings . . . 1869-1902/3.

Fisheries III.12; III.11

167
Sea fisheries of the United Kingdom. Statistical tables and memorandum . . . 1881/86-1902.

Incorporates information earlier given in its: Fish conveyed by railway. Return . . . 1878-1885.

Statistical tables III.8; Fisheries IV.9

168
Seamen's Savings Banks. Account of all deposits received and repaid by the Board of Trade . . . 1856-1914.

Savings banks IV.8; IV.10

169
Shipbuilding Credit Act 1964. Loans to shipowners. Account . . . 1964/65+.

170
Shipping casualties and deaths. Return . . . vessels registered in the United Kingdom. 1855+.

Title varies: Merchant shipping. Returns of shipping casualties . . .

Issued by Ministry of Transport, 1948-1962.

PP: 1855-1914/18.

NP: 1919/21+.

Not issued: 1939-1947; summary return for these years included in 1948 Return.

Wrecks IV.4; II.6

171
Sight tests. Report on the sight tests used in the mercantile marine . . . 1877/78-1913.

Similar figures later included in its: Mercantile marine – examinations for certificates of competency. Report . . . 1914-1920.

Colour blindness; Merchant shipping III.25

172
State of employment in the United Kingdom. Report . . . Oct., Dec. 1914, Feb. 1915.
Labour III.9

173
Statistical abstract for the British Empire . . . 1-11, 1889/1903-1899/1913.
Statistics

174
Statistical abstract for the principal and other foreign countries. 1-39, 1860/72-1901/12.
Statistical tables III.9; Statistics

175
Statistical tables relating to British colonies, possessions, and protectorates . . . 1-37, 1854-1912.
Title varies: 1854-1901, Statistical tables relating to the colonial and other possessions of the United Kingdom . . .
For similar statistics before 1854, see its: Tables of the revenue, population, commerce, etc., of the United Kingdom and its dependencies . . . 1820-1852.
Statistical tables III.2; Colonies III.35

176
Tables showing the progress of merchant shipping in the United Kingdom and the principal maritime countries. 1870-1913.
Statistical tables III.14; Merchant shipping IV.28

177
Tea and coffee. Memorandum and statistical tables showing the consumption of tea and coffee . . . and tables showing imports . . . 1900-1908.
Title varies.
Tea and coffee

178
Trade and navigation. Accounts relating to trade and navigation of the United Kingdom. Feb. 1848-Dec. 1964.
Superseded by its: Overseas trade accounts . . . Jan. 1965+. (NP)
Not issued: 1940-1945.
Trade IV.1(b); IV.52

179
Trade unions. Report by the Chief

Labour Correspondent of the Board of Trade . . . 1-17, 1887-1908/10.
Trades unions; Trade boards III.11

180
Tramway Orders Confirmation Bill. Copy of memorandum stating the nature of the proposals contained in the Provisional Orders included in the Tramway Orders Confirmation Bill. 1900-1904.
Tramways IV.2

181
Unemployment insurance. Report on the proceedings of the Board of Trade under Part II of the National Insurance Act 1911. 1, 1911/13.
No more issued.
Insurance, National Unemployment III.1

182
United Kingdom (trade, commerce and condition of people). Return . . . 1801/1902-1851/1914.
Trade IV.54

183
Wages and effects of deceased seamen. Account . . . 1884/85-1919/20.
Not issued: 1914/15-1917/18.
Merchant shipping IV.64; IV.29

184
Wages and hours of labour. Annual report on changes in rates of wages and hours of labour in the United Kingdom . . . 1-21, 1893-1913.
Wages

185
West Highland railway (extension from Banavic to Mallaig). Report . . . as to the condition and working of the Banavic to Mallaig railway, the rates and charges for traffic, and the receipts and expenditure . . . 1-13, 1901/2-1913/14.
Railways (Scotland)

**Board of Trade.
Commercial Intelligence Committee**

186
Report . . . on their proceedings . . . 1900/3-1913/18.
Trade III.9

Board of Trade.
Companies Registration Office

187
Joint stock companies. Return . . . 1859-1906.
> *Joint stock companies IV.1;*
> *Companies IV.4*

Board of Trade.
Department of Overseas Trade

188
Report on the economic and financial conditions . . . [of various countries]. 1-736, 1919-1939.
Title varies.
PP: 1-16, 1919-1920.
NP: 17-736, 1920-1939.
> *Indexed under names of countries*

Board of Trade.
London Traffic Branch

189
Report . . . 1-8, 1905/7-1915.
> *London III.20*

Board of Trade, Standards Department

190
Weights and Measures Acts. Report by the Board of Trade on their proceedings under the Weights and Measures Acts. 1866/67-1938.
PP: 1866/67-1915/20.
NP: 1921-1938.
> *Weights and measures*

Board of Trustees for the National Galleries of Scotland

191
Report . . . 1, 1907+.
Supersedes: Board of Manufactures in Scotland. National Gallery, etc. Annual Report . . .
PP: 1-14, 1907-1920/21.
NP: 15, 1921/22+.
> *National Gallery, etc. (Scotland)*

Boundary Commission for England

192
Periodical report. 1, 1954+.
Irregular.

193
Report . . . 1945+.
Irregular.
> *Elections*

Boundary Commission for Northern Ireland

194
Periodical report. 1, 1954+.
Irregular.

Boundary Commission for Scotland

195
Periodical report. 1, 1954+.
Irregular.

196
Report . . . 1947+.
Irregular.
> *Elections*

Boundary Commission for Wales

197
Periodical report. 1, 1954+.
Irregular.

198
Report . . . 1951.
No more issued.
> *Elections*

British Airports Authority

Established August 1965 under Airports Authority Act 1965.

199
Annual report and accounts . . . 1965/67+.

British Broadcasting Corporation

The Corporation was created January 1927 by Royal Charter.

200
Annual report and accounts . . . 1927+.
 Not issued: 1939-1944/45.
Broadcasting

British European Airways Corporation

Established August 1946 pursuant to Civil Aviation Act 1946.

201
Annual report and accounts . . . 1946/ 47+.
 Reports are to Ministry of Aviation until 1965/66, to Board of Trade 1966/ 67+.
Air III.5; Aviation, civil

British Film Fund Agency

Established by Cinematograph Films Act 1957.

202
Annual report and statement of accounts . . . 1, 1957/58+.
Cinematographs

British Museum

Formally established by an Act of 1753 to house Sir Hans Sloane's museum and library; the origins of the Museum, however, go back much further, to an Act of 1700 for the preservation of Robert Cotton's bequest.

203
Account of the income and expenditure of the British Museum . . . with a statement of the progress made in the arrangement and description of the collections . . . 1811-1920/21.
 Continued by its: Annual report of the general progress of the Museum . . . 1921-1938 (NP).
British Museum

British Overseas Airways Corporation

The Corporation was formed in 1940, but operated under the control of the *Air Ministry until April 1945.

204
Annual report and accounts . . . 1946/ 47+.
 Presented pursuant to Civil Aviation Act 1946, until 1965/66 to Ministry of Aviation, 1966/67+ to Board of Trade.
Air III.6; Aviation, civil

British Phosphate Commission

The Commission was set up by treaty with Australia and New Zealand in 1919.

205
Report and accounts . . . 1949/50+.
 Until 1948/49 accounts were provided in Exchequer and Audit Department's Trading accounts and balance sheets . . .
 1949/50 issued as British Phosphate Commission. Trading account and balance sheet . . . .
Phosphate Commission

British Railways Board

Board established under Transport Act 1962, assuming some of the functions of the *British Transport Commission.

206
Annual report and accounts. 1, 1963+.

British South Africa Company

Established and granted a Royal Charter in 1889 to promote trade and commerce in southern Africa, the Company was responsible for the administration of Southern and Northern Rhodesia until these territories became Crown colonies in 1923 and 1924 respectively.

207
Administrative revenue and expenditure

in Southern and Northern Rhodesia . . .
1912/13-1913/14.

Rhodesia

208
Financial statements . . . and estimates
. . . 1896/1900-1902/5.
    Dates shown are for Financial state-
ments; Estimates are for the following
year (e.g., 1903/6 Estimates accompany
1902/5 Financial statements). Estimates
were also issued separately for 1902/4.
        British South Africa Company;
                            Rhodesia

British South American Airways Corporation

Corporation established August 1946,
pursuant to Civil Aviation Act 1946.
Merged with *British Overseas Airways
Corporation in 1949.

209
Annual report and statement of accounts. 1946/47-1948/49.
                            Air III. 7

British Transport Commission

Commission was appointed by Minister
of Transport under Transport Act 1947.
Superseded in 1962 by *British Rail-
ways Board, *British Transport Docks
Board, *British Waterways Board, and
*London Transport Board.

210
Annual report and accounts . . . 1-15,
1948-1962.
                            Transport

British Transport Docks Board

Board established under Transport Act
1962, assuming some of the functions of
the *British Transport Commission.

211
Annual report and accounts. 1, 1963+.

British Waterways Board

Board established under Transport Act
1962, assuming some of the functions
of the *British Transport Commission.

212
Annual report and accounts. 1, 1963+.

Caledonian Canal Commission

213
Report . . . 1-115, 1803/4-1919/20.
                    Caledonian Canal

Cape of Good Hope. Royal Observatory

214
Report of the Astronomer . . . 1896-
1920.
    Later reports not issued as govern-
ment publications.
            Cape Colony II.12;
    Cape of Good Hope Observatory

Carpet Industry Training Board

Board established March 1966 under
Industrial Training Act 1964.

215
Report and statement of accounts . . .
1966+.

Catering Wages Commission

Established under the Catering Wages
Act 1943.

216
Annual report . . . 1-13, 1943/44-1956.
                            Catering

Central Control Board (Liquor Traffic)

Established 1915 by the Defence of the

Realm (Liquor Control) Regulations. Abolished by Licensing Act 1921, its powers passing to the *Home Office.

217
Defence of the Realm (Liquor Control) Regulations 1915. Central Control Board (Liquor Traffic). Report . . . 1-4, 1915/16-1918.
Continued by its: Defence of the Realm (Liquor Control) Regulations 1915. General Manager's report on the Carlisle Direct Control Area . . .
Licensing acts III.1

218
Defence of the Realm (Liquor Control) Regulations 1915. General Manager's report on the Carlisle and District Direct Control Area . . . 1918-1920.
Preceded by its: Defence of the Realm (Liquor Control) Regulations 1915. Central Control Board (Liquor Traffic). Report . . .
Superseded by: Home Office. State management districts. Annual report . . .
Licensing acts III.1, III.5

219
Statement of assets and liabilities . . . made by the General Managers. Dec. 1916-March 1919.
Licensing acts IV.1

Central Electricity Authority

Established in April 1948 as British Electricity Authority, with responsibility for Area Electricity Boards. Renamed in April 1955. Under Electricity Act 1957 superseded by two bodies: the *Central Electricity Generating Board and the *Electricity Council.

220
Report and statement of accounts. 1-10, 1947/49-1957.
1-7, 1947/49-1954/55 as British Electricity Authority.
Electricity

Central Electricity Generating Board

Established under Electricity Act 1957, superseding, with *Electricity Council, the *Central Electricity Authority.

221
Report and accounts . . . 1, 1958/59+.
Electricity

Central Health Services Council

Established under National Health Service Act 1946.

222
Report . . . 1948/49+.
Health

Central Land Board

Established by Town and Country Planning Act 1947. Dissolved in April 1959, its functions being transferred to the *Ministry of Housing and Local Government and the *Department of Health for Scotland, later the *Scottish Home and Health Department.

223
Report . . . 1-10, 1948/49-1957/58.
Later, this material is included in Reports of the Ministry of Housing and Local Government, and the Scottish Home and Health Department.
Land, etc. III.2

Central Midwives Board

224
Report . . . 1902/8-1938/39.
PP: 1902/8-1919/20.
NP: 1920/21-1938/39.
Midwives

Central Midwives Board for Scotland

225
Report . . . 1916/17-1937/38.

Earlier included in: Central Mid-
wives Board. Report.
PP: 1916/17-1918/19.
NP: 1919/20-1937/38.
Midwives (Scotland)

Central Office of Information

Formed April 1946, taking over a wide
range of duties from the Ministry of
Information, which was disbanded 30
March 1946. The Ministry did not pub-
lish reports of its work.

226
Annual report. 1-3, 1947/48-1949/50.
Information

Central Statistical Office

Established in 1940 to answer the need
for a coordinated collection of statistics,
which had previously been collected
by individual departments, it evolved
from the 1939 Central Economic Information Service.

227
Annual abstract of statistics. 1, 1840/53+.
  1-83 issued by Board of Trade, as
Statistical abstract for the United King-
dom; 84-85 by Treasury.
  PP: 1-83, 1840/53-1924/38.
  NP: 84, 1935/46+.
  Statistical tables III.1; Statistics II.3

228
United Kingdom balance of payments
. . . 1946/47+.
  Issued by Treasury, 1946/47-1959/
62.
  PP: 1946/47-1959/62.
  NP: 1963+.
  Finance III.4; Balance of payments

Central Training Council

Council established May 1964 under
Industrial Training Act 1964.

229
Report . . . 1, 1964/65+.

Central Transport Consultative Committee for Great Britain

Appointed pursuant to Transport Act
1947.

230
Annual report . . . 1949+.
Transport

Ceramics, Glass and Mineral Products Industry Training Board

Board established July 1965 under Industrial Training Act 1964.

231
Report and statement of accounts . . .
1965/66+.

Charity Commission

The modern Charity Commission was
established under the Charitable Trusts
Act 1853. It reported direct to the
Sovereign, and although its reports were
laid before Parliament, the lack of a
responsible Minister made the securing
of legislation difficult. The Commission
was reconstituted in 1960 by the Charities Act and now reports to the Home
Secretary.

232
Report of the Charity Commissioners
for England and Wales . . . 1-32, 1818-
1836/37; n.s., 1-107, 1853-1959; 1960+.
  PP: 1-32, 1818-1836/37; n.s., 1-86,
  1853-1938; 1960+.
  NP: 97-107, 1949-1959.
  Not issued: 87-96, 1939-1948.
Charities

Chemical and Allied Products Industry Training Board

Board established October 1967 under Industrial Training Act 1964.

233
Report and statement of accounts . . . 1967/68+.

Church Estates Commissioners

The Crown appoints two Commissioners, and the Archbishop of Canterbury one, to consider dealings in land by ecclesiastical corporations.

234
Report. 1-88, 1852-1938/39.
*Ecclesiastical Commission III.2;
Ecclesiastical affairs; Church estates*

Cinematograph Films Council

Council was appointed June 1938 under Cinematograph Films Act 1938, superseding an Advisory Committee.

235
Annual report . . . 1, 1938/39+.
Not issued: 2-7, 1939/40-1944/45.
Cinematographs

Civil Air Transport Industry Training Board

Board established March 1967 under Industrial Training Act 1964.

236
Report and statement of accounts . . . 1967+.

Civil Aviation Advisory Board

237
Report on the imperial air mail services

. . . 1, 1922.
No more issued.
Air III.14

Civil Service Commission

Established by Order in Council, 1855. The Civil Service is a department of the Treasury, and the Commissioners are appointed by the Treasury. Their duties include administration of the scheme of competitive examination for positions in the permanent government service, and the establishing of conditions of service.

238
Annual report. 1, 1855+.
PP: 1-65, 1855-1920.
NP: 66, 1921+.
Civil Service III.1; III.5

Coal Commission

Established under Coal Act 1938; dissolved by the Coal Industry Nationalisation Act 1946, its rights, etc., being transferred to the National Coal Board.

239
Accounts . . . 1938/39-1946.
Coal industry IV.6

Colombo Plan Consultative Committee

Established following the meeting in Colombo of Commonwealth Foreign Ministers in January 1950.

240
Colombo Plan for co-operative economic development in South and South-East Asia. Annual report of the Consultative Committee . . . 1, 1952+.
   1-10, 1952-1961, presented by Treasury; 11-12, 1962-1963, by Commonwealth Relations Office; 13, 1964+ by Ministry of Overseas Development.
Colombo Plan

**Colonial Development
Advisory Committee**

241
Interim report. 1-11, 1929/30-1939/40.
Colonies II. 7

Colonial Office

Colonial business became the responsibility of a Third Secretary of State in
the Home Office in 1801, though his
title at that date was Secretary of State
for War. His new duties rapidly pre-
dominated, and the title of Secretary of
State for the Colonies was in use by 1812.
Duties related to war were separated in
1854, when the Colonial Office took its
modern form. In 1966 the Colonial
Office and the Commonwealth Relations
Office were amalgamated to form the
*Commonwealth Office. This, in its
turn, was amalgamated in 1968 with the
*Foreign Office to form the *Foreign
and Commonwealth Office.

242
Africa. Blackwater fever in the tropical
African dependencies . . . Reports . . .
1911-1913.
Africa III.1(a)

243
Cameroons under United Kingdom administration. Report by H.M. Government . . . 1920/21-1959.
    1920/21-1938, Reports are to Coun-
cil of the League of Nations; 1947, to
the United Nations Trusteeship Council;
1948-1959, to the General Assembly of
the United Nations.
    PP: 1920/21.
    NP: 1922-1959.
    Not issued: 1939-1946.
Cameroons

244
Colonial reports . . . Annual . . . 1-1936,
1889-1938/39; 1946+.
    PP: 1-1071, 1889-1921.
    NP: 1072, 1921+.
Colonies III.1; II.1(a)

Note: The Colonial reports, Annual
series, that have appeared in the Ses-

sional Papers since 1900 are listed below, items 245-296. The Annual series
was preceded by the "Old series" of reports, which was subdivided in 1889 into
two series, Annual and Miscellaneous. In
noting first issue dates, the earliest date
of appearance in the "Old series" is
given where appropriate.
    No reports in the Annual series were
issued for the years 1940-1945. Responsibility for those reports still being
issued was assumed by the *Commonwealth Office in 1966 and by the *Foreign and Commonwealth Office in 1968.
However, all are listed here, so that the
entire series may appear in one place:

245
Ashanti. Report. 1905-1925/26.
    Continued in its: Gold Coast. Re-
port . . .
    PP: 1905-1919.
    NP: 1920-1925/26.
Ashanti

246
Bahama Islands. Report . . . 1887+.
    PP: 1887-1919/20.
    NP: 1920/21+.
    Not issued: 1939-1945.
Bahamas

247
Barbados. Report . . . 1887-1962/63.
    PP: 1887-1918/19.
    NP: 1919/20-1962/63.
    Not issued: 1940-1946.
Barbados

248
Basutoland. Report . . . 1887-1963.
    PP: 1887-1919/20.
    NP: 1920/21-1963.
    Not issued: 1939-1945.
Basutoland

249
Bechuanaland Protectorate. Report
. . . 1887/88-1965.
    PP: 1887/88-1919/20.
    NP: 1921/22-1965.
    Not issued: 1897/98-1901/2,1939-
1945.
Bechuanaland

250
Bermuda. Report . . . 1887+.

PP: 1887-1919.
NP: 1920+.
Not issued: 1939-1945.
Bermuda

251
British Guiana. Report . . . 1887-1961.
PP: 1887-1919.
NP: 1920-1961.
Not issued: 1939-1945.
Guiana, British

252
British Honduras. Report . . . 1887+.
PP: 1887-1919.
NP: 1920+.
Not issued: 1939-1945.
Honduras Colony;
Honduras, British

253
British New Guinea. Report . . . 1887-1899/1900.
New Guinea; Papua

254
British Solomon Islands. Report . . . 1897/98+.
PP: 1897/98-1919/20.
NP: 1921/22+.
Notissued: 1905/6-1911/12, 1913/14-1916/17, 1939-1947.
Solomon Islands

255
Brunei. Report . . . 1906-1960.
Later reports, by independent State of Brunei, not issued as British Government publications.
PP: 1906-1919.
NP: 1920-1960.
Not issued: 1907-1914, 1939-1945.
Straits Settlements

256
Cayman Islands. Report . . . 1905/6+.
1905/6, 1908/9, in Miscellaneous series; 1911/12+ in Annual series.
PP: 1905/6-1917/18.
NP: 1918/19+.
Not issued: 1906/7-1907/8, 1909-1911, 1938-1945.
Jamaica

257
Ceylon. Report . . . 1887-1938.

PP: 1887-1919.
NP: 1920-1938.
Ceylon

258
Christmas and Cocos-Keeling Islands. Report . . . 1897-1903.
Title varies.
Straits Settlements

259
Colonial Survey Committee. Annual report. 1905/6-1929.
PP: 1905/6-1913/14.
NP: 1914/23-1929.
Colonies II.17

260
Cyprus. Report . . . 1879-1959.
PP: 1879-1919/20.
NP: 1921-1959.
Not issued: 1939-1945.
Cyprus

261
Entomological research. Report . . . 1912/13-1914.
1912/13, Report of the Committee . . .
1914, Report of the Imperial Bureau of Entomology . . .
Entomological research

262
Falkland Islands. Report . . . 1887+.
PP: 1887-1918.
NP: 1919+.
Not issued: 1939-1946.
Falkland Islands

263
Federated Malay States. Report . . . 1889-1938.
States included: Negri Sembilan, Pahang, Perak, Selangor.
Later reports: 1947-1948 in Malayan Union Reports (NP); 1950-1956 in Federation of Malaya Reports (NP).
PP: 1889-1919.
NP: 1920-1938.
Straits Settlements; Malaya

264
Fiji. Report . . . 1887+.
PP: 1887-1919.

NP: 1920+.
Not issued: 1939-1946.
Fiji

265
Gambia. Report . . . 1886-1962/63.
PP: 1886-1919.
NP: 1920-1962/63.
Not issued: 1939-1945.
Gambia

266
Gibraltar. Report . . . 1887+.
PP: 1887-1919.
NP: 1920+.
Not issued: 1939-1945.
Gibraltar

267
Gilbert and Ellice Islands. Report . . .
1896/1900+.
PP: 1896/1900-1918/19.
NP: 1919/20+.
Not issued: 1938-1947.
Gilbert and Ellice Islands

268
Gold Coast. Report . . . 1888-1954.
PP: 1888-1919.
NP: 1920-1954.
Not issued: 1940-1945.
Gold Coast

269
Gold Coast (Northern Territories).
Report . . . 1901-1925/26.
Continued in its. Gold Coast. Report . . .
PP: 1901-1918.
NP: 1919-1925/26.
Gold Coast

270
Grenada. Report . . . 1887+.
PP: 1887-1919.
NP: 1920+.
Not issued: 1939-1947.
Grenada

271
Hong Kong. Report . . . 1887+.
PP: 1887-1919.
NP: 1920+.
Not issued: 1939-1945.
Hong Kong

272
Jamaica. Report . . . 1887-1961/62.
1887 includes Report on Turks
Islands, later issued separately.
PP: 1887-1919/20.
NP: 1920-1961/62.
Not issued: 1939-1945.
Jamaica

273
Kenya Colony and Protectorate. Report . . . 1900/1-1962.
1900/1-1918/19 as East Africa
Protectorate.
1900/1-1903/4 issued by Foreign
Office; 1904/5+ in Colonial Office
Annual series.
PP: 1900/1-1917/18.
NP: 1918/19-1962.
Not issued: 1902/3, 1939-1945.
Africa III.3(a)

274
Leeward Islands. Report . . . 1887-1953/54.
PP: 1887-1918/19.
NP: 1919/20-1953/54.
Not issued: 1938-1946.
Leeward Islands

275
Malta. Report . . . 1887-1920/21.
PP: 1887-1919/20.
NP: 1920/21.
Malta

276
Mauritius. Report . . . 1886-1967.
1886-1887 include Seychelles. Report . . . , later issued separately.
1886-1888, 1897-1908 include Rodrigues. Report . . . , issued separately
1889/90-1896.
PP: 1886-1919.
NP: 1920-1967.
Not issued: 1939-1945.
Mauritius

277
Nigeria. Report . . . 1915-1955.
PP: 1915-1919.
NP: 1920-1955.
Not issued: 1939-1945.
Nigeria

278
Northern Nigeria. Report . . . 1900/1-1913.

Continued in its: Nigeria. Report . . .
Nigeria

279
Nyasaland. Report . . . 1902/3-1962.
1902/3-1906/7 as British Central Africa Protectorate.
1902/3 issued by Foreign Office; 1903/4+ in Colonial Office Annual series.
PP: 1902/3-1918/19.
NP: 1919/20-1962.
Not issued: 1939-1945.
Nyasaland

280
Saint Helena. Report . . . 1887+.
PP: 1887-1919.
NP: 1920+.
Not issued: 1939-1946.
Saint Helena

281
Saint Lucia. Report . . . 1887+.
PP: 1887-1915/16.
NP: 1921+.
Not issued: 1916/17-1920, 1939-1945.
Saint Lucia

282
Saint Vincent. Report . . . 1887+.
PP: 1887-1919.
NP: 1920+.
Not issued: 1939-1945.
Saint Vincent

283
Seychelles. Report . . . 1888+.
Reports for 1886-1887 included in its: Mauritius. Report . . .
PP: 1888-1919.
NP: 1920+.
Not issued: 1938-1945.
Seychelles

284
Sierra Leone. Report . . . 1887-1958.
PP: 1887-1919.
NP: 1920-1958.
Not issued: 1939-1945.
Sierra Leone

285
Somaliland. Report . . . 1904/5-1958/59.
PP: 1904/5-1919/20.

NP: 1920-1958/59.
Not issued: 1938-1947.
Somaliland

286
Southern Nigeria. Report . . . 1898/99-1913.
1898/99 as Niger Coast Protectorate.
For later reports see its: Nigeria. Report . . .
Niger Territories; Nigeria

287
Southern Nigeria (Lagos). Report . . . 1887-1905.
Lagos

288
Straits Settlements. Report . . . 1887-1938.
Reports are for Malacca, Penang, and Singapore.
Later reports, all NP, for Singapore are published separately; for Malacca and Penang in Malayan Union Report 1947-1948, in Federation of Malaya Report 1950-1956.
PP: 1887-1919.
NP: 1920-1938.
Straits Settlements

289
Swaziland. Report . . . 1906/7-1966.
PP:1906/7-1919/20.
NP: 1920/21-1966.
Not issued: 1939-1945.
Swaziland

290
Tonga. Report . . . 1909+.
PP: 1909-1914/15.
NP: 1923/24+.
Not issued: 1915/16-1922/23,1939-1945.
Tongan Islands

291
Trinidad and Tobago. Report . . . 1887-1957.
PP: 1887-1919.
NP: 1920-1957.
Not issued: 1939-1945.
Trinidad and Tobago

292
Turks and Caicos Islands. Report . . .
1888+.
Report for 1887 included in its:
Jamaica. Report . . .
PP: 1888-1919.
NP: 1920+.
Not issued: 1939-1945.
Jamaica

293
Uganda. Report . . . 1901-1961.
1901-1903/4 issued by Foreign
Office; 1904/5+ in Colonial Office
Annual series.
PP: 1901-1918/19.
NP: 1920-1961.
Not issued: 1939-1945.
Uganda

294
Unfederated Malay States. Reports
. . . 1910-1926.
Reports are for Johore, Kedah
and Perlis, Kelantan, Trengganu.
Earlier, separate Reports (PP),
1909, for Kedah and Perlis, Kelantan.
Later, separate Reports for each
state (NP), 1927/28 or 1928 to
1938 or 1938/39; 1947-1948 in Malayan Union Report; 1950-1956 in Federation of Malaya Report.
PP: 1910-1919.
NP: 1920-1926.
Malaya

295
Wei-Hai-Wei. Report . . . 1902-1929.
PP: 1902-1919.
NP: 1920-1929.
Wei-Hai-Wei

296
Zanzibar. Report . . . 1913-1959/60.
PP: 1913-1919.
NP: 1920-1959/60.
Not issued: 1939-1945.
Zanzibar

297
Colonial reports . . . Miscellaneous . . .
1-93, 1891-1921.
PP: 1-92, 1891-1920.
NP: 93, 1921.
Colonies III.1; II.1(b)

298
Colonial research. Reports of the Colon-
ial Research Council, Colonial Products
Research Council . . . 1943/44-1960/61.

Title varies: 1943/44-1944/45, Report of Colonial Research Committee
(later Council).
1945/46 includes Reports of various
other bodies, including 2nd Report of
Colonial Products Research Council, 1st
Report of which was separately published in PP. Additional agencies added
at various dates.
PP: 1943/44-1944/45, 1946/47-1960/
61.
NP: 1945/46.
Colonies II.14

299
Colonial territories. 1937/38-1960/61.
Title varies: 1937/38-1947/48, The
Colonial empire.
A single report was issued for 1939/
47.
Colonies II.10, II.18

300
Dominions. 1-16, 1910-1914.
Colonies II.23

301
East Africa Protectorate. Report on
veterinary bacteriological work . . .
1906/7-1907/8.
In its Miscellaneous series.
Title varies: 1906/7: . . . Annual re-
port of the Veterinary Department.
A Report for 1905/6 is included in its:
East Africa Protectorate. Report . . .
1905/6 (see entry for: Kenya Colony
and Protectorate. Report . . .).
Africa III.3(p)

302
Importation of spirituous beverages in
British colonies and protectorates in
Africa and the import duties levied
thereon. Report . . . 1920-1938.
Title varies.
Africa IV.1(b)

303
Return showing the number of death
sentences and executions in British
Crown colonies and protectorates . . .
1908-1914.
Capital punishment

304
Tanganyika under United Kingdom administration. Report by H.M. Government . . . 1920-1960.
1920-1938, Reports are to Çouncil

of the League of Nations; 1947, to the United Nations Trusteeship Council; 1948-1960, to the General Assembly of the United Nations.
PP: 1920-1921.
NP: 1922-1960.
Not issued: 1939-1946.

Tanganyika

305
Togoland under United Kingdom administration. Report by H.M. Government . . . 1920/21-1955.
1920/21-1938, Reports are to Council of the League of Nations; 1947, to the United Nations Trusteeship Council; 1948-1955, to the General Assembly of the United Nations.
PP: 1920/21.
NP: 1922-1955.
Not issued: 1939-1946.

Togoland

306
West Africa. Return of vital statistics of non-native officials . . . 1911-1920.

Africa IV.3(d)

Colonial Office. Advisory Committee for the Tropical Diseases Research Fund

307
Tropical Diseases Research Fund. Report. 1906-1914.

Tropical diseases

Colonial Office. Colonial Research Committee

308
Annual report. 1920-1926/28.
PP: 1920.
NP: 1923-1926/28.
Not issued: 1921-1922.

Colonies II.14

Colonial Office. Dominions Department

309
Report . . . 1909/10-1913/14.

In: Colonial Office. Dominions (nos. 2, 6, 12, 14, 16).

Colonies II.23

Colonial Products Research Council

310
Annual report . . . 1, 1943/44.
Later reports included in: Colonial Office. Colonial research . . . 1944/45-1960/61.

Colonies II.14

Colonisation Board

311
Colonisation of crofters. Report of H.M. Commissioners appointed to carry out a scheme of colonisation in the Dominion of Canada of crofters and cottars from the Western Highlands and Islands of Scotland . . . 1-15, 1890-1906.

Crofters and cottars;
Crofters(Scotland)

Commission for the New Towns

Commission established October 1961, under New Towns Act 1959, to take over administration of new towns in England and Wales from those Development Corporations whose purposes had been achieved or substantially achieved.

312
New Towns Act 1965. Report of the Commission for the New Towns . . . 1962/63+.

Commissioners of Church Temporalities in Wales

The Commission was established by the Welsh Church Act 1914, and dissolved in December 1947, when final distributions of property had been made.

313
Report. 1-24, 1914/15-1938.

Church of England (Wales)

314
Welsh Church Commission. Welsh Church
Act 1914. Accoûnts . . . 1914/15-1947.
Church of England (Wales)

Commissioners of Customs

Separate Boards of Customs and of
Excise were established for England as
early as 1643, for Scotland in 1707. In
1823 these four Boards and the Irish
Revenue Board were reconstituted to
form the Customs Board and the Excise Board, each with responsibility
for the entire United Kingdom. The
Customs Board became the *Customs
and Excise in 1909, when responsibility
for excise duties was transferred from
the *Inland Revenue Department.

315
Report . . . 1-53, 1856/57-1908/9.
    Superseded by: Customs and Excise.
Report . . .
Customs

**Committee on Manpower Resources
for Science and Technology**

316
Report on the triennial manpower survey
of engineers, technologists, scientists and
technical supporting staff. 1, 1956+.
    Title and issuing agency vary:
    1. Ministry of Labour & Advisory
       Council on Scientific Policy. Sci-
       entific and engineering manpower
       in Great Britain.
    2. Advisory Council on Scientific
       Policy. Committee on Scientific
       Manpower. Scientific and engineer-
       ing manpower in Great Britain.
    3. Advisory Council on Scientific
       Policy. Committee on Scientific
       Manpower. Scientific and tech-
       nological manpower in Great Bri-
       tain.
PP: 2, 1959+.
NP: 1, 1956.

**Committee on the Grant of Honours,
Decorations and Medals**

317
Reports . . . 1942/43+.
    Irregular.
Medals

Commonwealth Agricultural Bureaux

Originally the Imperial Agricultural Bureaux; the name of the agency was
changed to its present form in January
1948.

318
Commonwealth Agricultural Bureaux Review Conference. Report of proceedings
. . . 1946+.
    A Conference has normally been held
every five years since 1930, but no reports were published before 1946.
Colonies II.26; Agriculture III

**Commonwealth Development
Corporation**

Established under Overseas Resources
Development Act 1948 as Colonial Development Corporation. Name of agency
changed 1963.

319
Annual report and statement of ac-
counts . . . 1, 1948+.
Colonies II.9

**Commonwealth Immigrants
Advisory Council**

320
Report . . . 1-4, 1963-1965.
    Irregular.

Commonwealth Office

Formed in 1966 by the amalgamation

of the *Colonial Office and the Commonwealth Relations Office. In 1968 it was amalgamated with the *Foreign Office to form the *Foreign and Commonwealth Office.

321
Commonwealth Prime Ministers' meeting. Final communiqué. 1962+.
    Irregular.
    Earlier, see: Imperial Conference of Prime Ministers . . .

Commonwealth Scholarship Commission

Constituted in December 1959 by the Commonwealth Scholarship Act, to administer a scheme for the establishment of 1,000 scholarships and fellowships for postgraduate study and research, half of which were to be in the United Kingdom.

322
Annual report. 1, 1959/60+.

Commonwealth War Graves Commission

Appointed by Royal Warrant in May 1917 as the Imperial War Graves Commission. The name of the Commission was changed in 1959.

323
Annual report . . . 1, 1919/20+.
    1-40, 1919/20-1958/59, as Imperial War Graves Commission.
    PP: 1, 1919/20.
    NP: 2, 1920/21+.
                                    War graves

Congested Districts Board for Scotland

Established under the Congested Districts (Scotland) Act 1897, to administer sums available for the improvement of such districts. Its powers were transferred in 1912 to the Board of Agriculture for Scotland.

324
Report . . . 1-14, 1897/98-1911/12.
                Congested districts (Scotland)

Construction Industry Training Board

Established July 1964 under Industrial Training Act 1964.

325
Report and statement of accounts . . . 1964/65+.

Cotton and Allied Textiles Industry Training Board

Established July 1966 under Industrial Training Act 1964.

326
Report and statement of accounts . . . 1966/67+.

Council for Scientific Policy

The Council was established under the Science and Technology Act 1965, superseding the *Advisory Council on Scientific Policy.

327
Report on science policy. 1, 1966+.
    Irregular.

Council for Wales and Monmouthshire

Established in April 1949, following a House of Commons debate on Welsh affairs in November 1948, to advise the Home Secretary on matters pertaining to Wales. Dissolved in 1966, most of its work in the economic field being taken over by the Welsh Economic Council.

328
Memorandum . . . on its activities . . . 1-4, 1950-1959.
                Wales and Monmouthshire

29

329
Report . . . 1955-1966.
    Irregular reports on various subjects.
    Earlier, see its: Memorandum . . .
                  Wales and Monmouthshire

Council on Tribunals

Constituted in 1959, pursuant to the
Tribunals and Inquiries Act 1958. The
Council consists of 10 to 15 members
appointed by the Lord Chancellor and
the Secretary of State for Scotland;
there is also a Scottish Committee appointed by the latter.

330
Annual report . . . 1959+.
    PP: 1967+.
    NP: 1959-1966.

County Courts

331
Returns from every county court in
England and Wales of the total number
of plaints, etc., entered in each court
. . . 1847/48-1921.
    PP: 1847/48-1914.
    NP: 1915-1921.
              County courts IV.8; IV.3

Criminal Injuries Compensation Board

Established September 1964 to consider
applications for compensation from vic-
tims of crimes of violence.

332
Report. Accounts . . . 1, 1964/65+.

Criminal Law Revision Committee

Appointed by Warrant, February 1959.

333
Report . . . 1, 1959+.
               Criminal law

Crofters' Commission

Set up under the Crofters Holdings
(Scotland) Act 1886. Replaced in 1912
by the Scottish Land Court.

334
Annual report . . . 1886/87-1911/12.
    Continued by: Scottish Land Court.
Report . . .
              Crofters and cottars;
              Crofters (Scotland)

Crown Agents Office

The Crown Agents act as business agents
in the United Kingdom for the governments of Crown colonies and protectorates.

335
Accounts of the Crown Agents Office
funds. 1900/2-1919.
    Not issued: 1903-1908.
              Colonies III.11

Crown Estate Commissioners

Established as the Commissioners of
Woods, Forests and Land Revenues by
an Act of 1810, replacing the Surveyor
General of Land Revenues of the Crown
and the Surveyor General of H.M. Woods,
Forests, etc. In 1924 the majority of
Crown lands were transferred to the
Forestry Commission, and the Com-
missioners were renamed Commissioners
of Crown Lands. This body was recon-
structed under its present title by the
Crown Estate Act 1956.

336
Crown Estate abstract accounts . . .
1851/52+.
      Woods, forests and land revenues;
         Crown lands; Crown Estate

337
Report . . . 1-117, 1812-1938/39; 1956/
57+.

PP: 1-98, 1812-1919/20.
NP: 99-117, 1920/21-1938/39; 1956/57+.
Not issued: 1939/40-1955/56.
Woods, forests and land revenues

Customs and Excise

Established by a 1909 Order in Council under the Finance Act 1908. This Order replaced the *Commissioners of Customs and transferred the responsibility for excise duties and old age pensions from the *Inland Revenue Department.

338
Annual statement of the trade of the United Kingdom with Commonwealth countries and foreign countries . . . 1853+.
 1904-1913 have Supplement.
 Issued by Board of Trade to 1926, v. 3.
 PP: 1853-1920.
 NP: 1921+.
Trade IV.1(a); IV.7

339
Report of the Commissioners of H.M. Customs and Excise . . . 1, 1909/10+.
 Supersedes: Commissioners of Customs. Report . . .
 Not issued: 31-35, 1939/40-1943/44; a summary for these years is included in the 1944/45 Report.
Customs

340
Wines imported. Return of the quantity of foreign wines . . . which were imported . . . 1801-1914.
 Irregular.
 Title varies.
Wine; Wines and spirits

Decimal Currency Board

Established by Decimal Currency Act 1967.

341
Annual report . . . 1, 1967/68+.

Delegates to International Hydrographic Conferences

342
North Sea fishery investigation. Reports of the British delegates attending the meetings of the International Council for the Exploration of the Sea . . . 1-8, 1899-1909.
 Reports 1-2, 1899-1901, were made to the Foreign Office; 3, 1902, to the Board of Trade; 4-8, 1903/4-1909, to the Board of Agriculture and Fisheries.
 For other North Sea fishery investigation Reports, see Fishery Board for Scotland, and Marine Biological Association of the United Kingdom.
Fisheries III.10(a)

Delegation to the International Labour Conference

343
International Labour Conference . . . Report by the delegates of H.M. Government in the United Kingdom . . . 6th-47th sessions, 1924-1963.
 PP: 6-14, 1924-1930; 25-47, 1941-1963.
 NP: 15-17, 1931-1933.
 Not issued: 1-5, 1919-1923; 18-24, 1934-1938.
Treaties II.91;
International Labour Organisation

Delegation to the International Penitentiary Congress

344
Report on the proceedings . . . 5-8, 1895-1910.
 Name of Congress varies: International Penal and Prison Congress.
 Not issued: 1-4, 1872-1890.
Prisons II.8

Delegation to the League of Nations

345
League of Nations. Assembly. Report of British delegates . . . 3rd-20th sessions, 1922-1939. /

In Foreign and Colonial Office. Miscellaneous papers.
Not issued: 1-2, 1920-1921.
League of Nations III.2

346
League of Nations. Council. Report by . . . (British representatives) . . . 25th-67th sessions, 1923-1931/32.
In Foreign and Colonial Office. Miscellaneous papers.
Not issued: 1-24, 38, 60-61, 64-66.
League of Nations III.7

Department of Agriculture and Fisheries for Scotland

Established 1912 as the Board of Agriculture for Scotland, under the Small Landholders (Scotland) Act 1911, assuming the powers of the *Congested Districts Board for Scotland, and the powers in Scotland of the *Board of Agriculture and Fisheries. It was replaced in January 1929, under the Reorganisation of Offices (Scotland) Act 1928, by the Department of Agriculture for Scotland. The present title dates from 1960, when responsibility for fisheries in Scotland was transferred from the *Scottish Home Department.

347
Agricultural statistics, Scotland . . . 1912+.
1939/44 and 1945/49 each covered by a single report.
PP: 1912-1920.
NP: 1921+.
Agriculture (Scotland) IV.5

348
Agriculture in Scotland. Report . . . 1-27, 1912-1938/39; 1939/48+.
Agriculture (Scotland) III.1

349
Fisheries of Scotland. Report . . . 1872-1881; n.s., 1-57, 1882-1938; 1939/48+.
1872-1938 issued by Fishery Board for Scotland; 1939/48 by Scottish Home Department, to which the powers of Fishery Board for Scotland were transferred in September 1939.
Fisheries (Scotland) III

Department of Education and Science

Established April 1964, assuming all the functions of the *Ministry of Education and certain other responsibilities relating to universities.

350
Education and science in . . . Being a report of the Department of Education and Science. 1964+.
Supersedes: Ministry of Education. Education in . . . Report of the Ministry of Education for England and Wales. 1947-1963.
Title varies: 1964-1966, Education in . . .

351
Health of the school child. Annual report of the Chief Medical Officer . . . 1, 1908+.
PP: 1908-1920.
NP: 1921+.
Education and schools III.22

Department of Education and Science. Reviewing Committee on the Export of Works of Art.

352
Export of works of art. Report of the Reviewing Committee appointed by the Chancellor of the Exchequer in December, 1952. 1, 1952/54+.
To 1963/64, Reports were made to the Treasury.
Fine art

Department of Employment and Productivity

Established 1968, assuming all the functions of the *Ministry of Labour.

353
International Labour Conference. Proposed action by H.M. Government . . . on instruments adopted at . . . the International Labour Conference. 5th session, 1923+.
Treaties II.91; International Labour Organisation

354

Offices, Shops and Railway Premises Act 1963. Report by the Secretary of State for Employment and Productivity . . . 1, 1963/64+.

Department of Employment and Productivity. Factory Inspectorate

355

Annual report of H.M. Chief Inspector of Factories . . . 1834+.

Half-yearly, 1838-1877.

Title varies: Factories and workshops. Annual report . . .

Issued by Home Office, 1834-1940; by Ministry of Labour, 1941-1966.

Factories

356

Industrial health. Annual report of the Chief Inspector of Factories on industrial health. 1957+.

Issued by the Ministry of Labour, 1957-1966.

Health

Department of Health for Scotland

Established January 1929 by the Reorganisation of Offices (Scotland) Act, replacing the *Scottish Board of Health. In April 1959 it assumed the powers in Scotland of the dissolved *Central Land Board. In 1962 it was merged with the *Scottish Home Department to form the *Scottish Home and Health Department, some of its functions being transferred to the newly established *Scottish Development Department.

357

Counties, burghs, and parishes in Scotland. Return . . . of the areas, population and valuation . . . 1893/94-1936/37.

Irregular.

Issued by Local Government Board for Scotland, 1893/94-1915; by Scottish Board of Health, 1916-1928.

PP: 1893/94-1920.

NP: 1921-1936/37.

Local government (Scotland) IV.2

358

Report . . . 1929-1961.

Supersedes: Scottish Board of Health. Annual report.

Summary reports only issued for 1939/41 and 1942/45.

1949-1955 includes: Scottish Health Services Council. Report . . . , later issued separately, NP.

1960, 1961, in two parts: I. Health and welfare services; II. Housing, planning and environment.

Part I continued by: Scottish Home and Health Department. Health and welfare services in Scotland.

Health, public (Scotland) III;
Health (Scotland) II

Department of Scientific and Industrial Research

Set up December 1916 under a Committee of the Privy Council, the Department rapidly assumed a wide range of responsibilities. The Department of Scientific and Industrial Research Act 1956 placed it under an executive body, the Council for Scientific and Industrial Research. It was dissolved by the Science and Technology Act 1965, its activities being assumed by other government departments and by the *Science Research Council.

359

Report of the Research Council . . . 1915/16-1964.

Title varies.

Not issued: 1938-1948; review of these years included in 1947/48 Report.

Research;
Scientific and industrial research

Development Commission

Established by the Development and Road Improvement Acts 1909 and 1910, to consider and report to the Treasury on all applications for advances from the Development Fund. Its functions were much reduced following the creation in 1919 of the *Forestry Commission and the *Ministry of Transport.

360

Report of the Development Commis-
sioners . . . 1, 1910/11+.
   PP: 1-11, 1910/11-1920/21; 13, 1922/
23+.
   NP: 12, 1921/22.
   Not issued: 1939/40-1959/60; series
numbering continues unbroken.
*Development and
Road Improvement Fund*

Disposal and Liquidation Commission

Set up in 1920 to handle disposal of
surplus government property following
the 1914-1918 War. The Commission
ceased to exist in March 1924 under the
Ministry of Munitions and Shipping
(Cessation) Act 1921.

361

Progress report on disposal of surplus
government property and on liquidation
. . . 1-5, 1920/21-1923/24.
   1920/21 Report issued by Ministry
of Munitions.
   Title varies: Disposal of surplus government property. Statement of receipts . . .
Munitions III.10

Dominions Office

Set up in July 1925 to take over from
the *Colonial Office business connected
with the self-governing dominions and
business relating to the *Imperial Conference. In July 1947 it was renamed
the Commonwealth Relations Office,
which evolved in 1966 into the *Commonwealth Office by amalgamation with
the *Colonial Office.

362

Newfoundland. Annual report by the
Commission of Government . . . 1935-
1938.
Newfoundland

East Midlands Electricity Board

Established under the Electricity Act
1947.

363

Report and accounts . . . 1, 1948/49+.
Electricity

East Midlands Gas Board

Established under the Gas Act 1948.

364

Annual report and accounts . . . 1, 1949/
50+.
Gas

Eastern Electricity Board

Established under the Electricity Act
1947.

365

Report and accounts . . . 1, 1948/49+.
Electricity

Eastern Gas Board

Established under the Gas Act 1948.

366

Annual report and accounts . . . 1,
1949/50+.
Gas

**Ecclesiastical Commissioners
for England**

Constituted in 1836 to recommend
schemes for church revenues, distribution of episcopal duties, etc. The Commission and *Queen Anne's Bounty
Board were dissolved in 1948, being replaced by the Church Commissioners.

367

Report . . . with . . . appendix . . . 1-91,
1846-1938/39.
Ecclesiastical Commission

**Economic Advisory Council.
Committee on Locust Control**

368
Report . . . 1929/30-1937.
    Name of Committee varies slightly.
Locusts

Edinburgh. Royal Observatory

369
Annual report of the Astronomer Royal
for Scotland, 1-49, 1891-1938/39.
    PP: 1-31, 1891-1920/21.
    NP: 32-49, 1921/22-1938/39.
Edinburgh

Edinburgh. Royal Scottish Museum

370
Report. 1901-1921/22.
    1901-1903 as Edinburgh Museum of
Science and Art.
    Earlier reports in: Department of
Science and Art. Annual report.
    PP: 1901-1907.
    NP: 1908-1921/22.
    Not issued: 1915-1919.
Museums III.4, III.6

Edinburgh. University

371
Annual report on the state of the fin-
ances . . . 1889/90-1913/14.
Universities and colleges (Scotland)

372
Annual statistical report . . . 1898/99-
1913/14.
Universities and colleges (Scotland)

Electricity Council

Established 1958, superseding, with the
*Central Electricity Generating Board,
the *Central Electricity Authority. The
Council is responsible for the 12 Area
Electricity Boards established in 1948.

373
Report and accounts . . . 1, 1958/59+.
Electricity

**Electricity Supply Industry
Training Board**

Established June 1965 under Industrial
Training Act 1964.

374
Report and statement of accounts . . .
1965/66+.

Emigrants' Information Office

Established 1886 to give advice to in-
tending emigrants to British colonies
and dominions. Replaced in 1919 by
the *Oversea Settlement Office.

375
Report . . . 1886/87-1914.
    Title of 1st Report: Papers relating
to the work of the Emigrants' Infor-
mation Office.
    Superseded by: Oversea Settlement
Office. Report . . .
Emigration IV.7; II.1

Empire Marketing Board

Board was established May 1926; abolished 1933.

376
Note on the work and finance of the
Board . . . 1926/27-1926/32.
    Note also NP Annual reports of
Board, 1926/27-1932/33 in Empire Mar-
keting Board Reports.
Empire Marketing Board

Engineering Industry Training Board

Established July 1964 under Industrial Training Act 1964.

377
Report and statement of accounts . . . 1964/65+.

Exchequer and Audit Department

Established by the Exchequer and Audit Department Act 1866, the Comptroller and Auditor General assuming the duties of the Comptroller General of the Exchequer (established 1834) and the Commissioners for auditing the public accounts (established 1785).

378
Agricultural Research Fund. Accounts . . . 1956/57-1963/64.
    Fund constituted by Agricultural Research Act 1956; administered by Agricultural Research Council.
Agriculture IV

379
Air Corporations Acts . . . Advances to Air Corporations. Account . . . 1962/63+.
    Continues its: Finance Act 1956. Advances to nationalised industries and undertakings (Minister of Aviation), Accounts . . .

380
Air services. Appropriation account . . . 1917/18-1963/64.
    From 1964/65, Appropriation accounts for all the fighting Services are combined in its: Defence accounts . . .
Air IV.2; Air Force III

381
Airports Authority Act 1965. Advances to the British Airports Authority. Account . . . of the sums received by the Board of Trade from the Consolidated Fund and from the British Airports Authority . . . 1966/67+.

382
American aid and European payments. Accounts of the Special Account, the American Aid (Agreed Schemes) Deposit Account, etc. . . . 1948/49-1958/59.
    Title varies, including various Accounts.
    Transactions on the first two Accounts were completed 1958/59; the remainder were in future to be published as appendices to the Appropriation Accounts of the Departments concerned.
United States of America; American and European payments

383
Army appropriation account . . . 1851/52-1963/64.
    From 1964/65, Appropriation accounts for all the fighting Services are combined in its: Defence accounts . . .
Army IV.6; IV.4

384
Army Clothing Factory. Annual accounts . . . with the report of the Comptroller and Auditor-General . . . 1886/87-1918/19.
Army V.20; V.9

385
Army (Ordnance Factories). Manufacturing accounts . . . 1886/87-1923/24.
    Title varies: Army (Ordnance Factories). Annual accounts . . .
    From 1924/25 included in its: Army (Royal Ordnance Factories) accounts. Appropriation account . . .
Ordnance and small arms IV.1; Ordnance factories II

386
Army (Royal Ordnance Factories) accounts. Appropriation account of the Royal Ordnance Factories and the Manufacturing account . . . 1888/89-1963/64.
    See also its: Army (Ordnance Factories). Manufacturing accounts . . . , issued separately, 1886/87-1923/24.
    From 1964/65, Appropriation accounts for all the fighting Services are combined in its: Defence accounts.
    Not issued: 1940/41-1959/60.
Ordnance and small arms III.2; Ordnance factories I.2

387
Atomic Energy Authority Act 1954. Accounts . . . Balance sheet of the United Kingdom Atomic Energy Authority . . .

and accounts for the year . . . 1954/55-1964/65.

From 1965/66 appended to: United Kingdom · Atomic Energy Authority. Atomic Energy Authority Act 1954. Report and accounts . . .

Atomic energy

388
China Indemnity Fund. Account . . . 1925/26-1931/32.

China IV.13

389
Civil appropriation accounts . . . Appropriation accounts of the sums granted by Parliament for Civil Services . . . 1921/22+.

Continues, in part, its: Civil Services and Revenue Departments. Appropriation accounts . . .

1921/22-1961/62, separate Accounts issued for Revenue Departments. 1962/63+, Accounts for Revenue Departments included in this title.

*Civil Service and Revenue
Departments IV.2;
Appropriation accounts*

390
Civil appropriation accounts (Class X, War services) . . . 1942/43-1944/45.

Continues its: Civil appropriation accounts (Unclassified Votes) . . .

*Civil Service and Revenue
Departments IV.12*

391
Civil appropriation accounts (Unclassified Votes). Appropriation accounts of the sums granted by Parliament· for Civil Services, Unclassified Votes . . . 1940/41-1941/42.

Continued by its: Civil appropriation accounts (Class X, War services) . . .

*Civil Service and Revenue
Departments IV.10*

392
Civil Contingencies Fund. Accounts . . . 1816+.

Civil contingencies

393
Civil Services and Revenue Departments. Appropriation accounts . . . 1861/62-1920/21.

From 1921/22 continued by two series, its: Civil appropriation accounts . . . , and its: Revenue Departments. Appropriation accounts . . .

*Civil Service and Revenue
Departments IV.7; IV.2*

394
Coal Industry Acts 1946 to 1965. Account of the sums issued out of and received from the Consolidated Fund . . . and of the sums received . . . from the National Coal Board . . . 1946/47+.

Coal

395
Colonial Development Fund. Abstract account . . . 1930/31-1940.

Colonies III.6

396
Consolidated Fund. Abstract account . . . 1866/67+.

Consolidated Fund

397
Cunard Insurance Fund. Account . . . 1931/32-1953/54.

Cunard

398
Czecho-Slovak Refugee Fund. Account . . . 1939/40+.

Title varies: 1939/40-1949/50, Czecho-Slovak Financial Claims Fund and Czecho-Slovak Refugee Fund. Accounts . . .

Czecho-Slovak Financial Claims Fund was wound up in 1950.

Czechoslovakia

399
Defence accounts . . . Accounts of the Defence Services . . . comprising (1) Appropriation accounts . . . for Defence Services . . . (2) Production accounts of the Navy Department . . . (3) Manufacturing account of the Royal Ordnance Factories . . . 1964/65+.

Continues its separate accounts previously issued for the Ministry of Defence and the three fighting Services.

400
Development Fund accounts . . . Abstract account . . . 1910/11+.

*Development and Road Improvement
Fund; Development Commission*

401
Electricity and Gas Act 1963. Advances to the Electricity Council and the Gas Council (Minister of Power). Account . . . 1963/64+.

Continues its: Finance Act 1956. Advances to nationalised industries and undertakings (Minister of Power). Account . . .

402
Electricity and Gas Act 1963. Advances to the North of Scotland Hydro-Electric Board and the South of Scotland Electricity Board . . . Account . . . 1963/64+.

Continues its: Finance Act 1956. Advances to nationalised industries and undertakings (Secretary of State for Scotland). Account . . .   1956/57-1962/63.

403
Finance Act 1956. Advances to nationalised industries and undertakings (Minister of Aviation). Accounts . . . 1959/60-1961/62.

Continues its: Finance Act 1956. Transport (Railway Finances) Act 1957. Advances to nationalised industries and undertakings (Minister of Transport and Civil Aviation). Accounts . . .

Continued by its: Air Corporations Acts, 1949 to 1966. Advances to Air Corporations. Account . . .

404
Finance Act 1956. Advances to nationalised industries and undertakings (Minister of Power). Account . . . 1956/57-1962/63.

Continued by its: Electricity and Gas Act 1963. Advances to the Electricity Council and the Gas Council (Minister of Power). Account . . . 1963/64+.
Nationalised industries

405
Finance Act 1956. Advances to nationalised industries and undertakings (Secretary of State for Scotland). Account . . . 1956/57-1962/63.

Continued by its: Electricity and Gas Act 1963. Advances to the North of Scotland Hydro-Electric Board and the South of Scotland Electricity Board . . .

Account . . . 1963/64+.
Nationalised industries

406
Finance Act 1956. Transport (Railway Finances) Act 1957. Advances to nationalised industries and undertakings (Minister of Transport). Accounts . . . 1959/60-1962/63.

Continues its: Finance Act 1956. Transport (Railway Finances) Act 1957. Advances to nationalised industries and undertakings (Minister of Transport and Civil Aviation). Accounts . . .

Continued by its: Transport Act 1962. Loans to nationalised transport undertakings (Minister of Transport). Account . . .

407
Finance Act 1956. Transport (Railway Finances) Act 1957. Advances to nationalised industries and undertakings (Minister of Transport and Civil Aviation). Accounts . . . 1956/57-1958/59.

Continued by its: Finance Act 1956. Advances to nationalised industries and undertakings (Minister of Aviation). Accounts . . . and by its: Finance Act 1956. Transport (Railway Finances) Act 1957. Advances to nationalised industries and undertakings (Minister of Transport). Accounts . . .
Nationalised industries

408
Funds in court in England and Wales. Accounts of the receipts and payments of the Accountant-General of the Supreme Court, in respect of the funds of suitors of the Supreme Court and of the County Courts . . . 1965/66+.

Presented pursuant to Administration of Justice Act 1965, superseding: National Debt Office. County Courts. Accounts . . . and: National Debt Office. Supreme Court of Judicature. Account

409
Harbours Act 1964. Loans to the National Ports Council and Statutory Harbour Authorities (Minister of Transport) Account . . . 1965/66+.

410
Highlands and Islands Development (Scot-

land) Act 1965. Account . . . of the Highlands and Islands Development Board . . . 1965/66+.

411
House of Commons Members' Contributory Pension Fund. Accounts . . . 1964/66+.

412
Industrial Organisation and Development Act 1947. Iron casting industry (scientific research levy). Account . . . 1967/68+.
Presented under Iron Casting Industry Order 1967 (S.I. 1967 no. 981).

413
Industrial Organisation and Development Act 1947. Lace furnishings industry (export promotion levy). Account . . . 1951/52-1957/58.
From 1958/59 incorporated in its: Industrial Organisation and Development Act 1947. Lace industry (levy.), etc. Account . . . (Title varies, including several levies; latest title: Wool textile industry (scientific research levy), etc. . . . Accounts . . .)
Lace industry

414
Industrial Organisation and Development Act 1947. Meat industry (scientific research levy). Account . . . 1963/64-1967/68.

415
Industrial Organisation and Development Act 1947. Wool textile industry (export promotion levy). Account . . . 1950/51-1957/58.
From 1958/59 incorporated in its: Industrial Organisation and Development Act 1947. Lace industry (levy), etc. Account . . . (Title varies, including several levies; latest title: Wool textile industry (scientific research levy), etc. . . . Accounts . . .)
Wool

416
Industrial Organisation and Development Act 1947. Wool textile industry (scientific research levy), etc. . . . accounts . . . 1949/50+.
Accounts of several levies; contents vary. Initially, only Account of Lace industry levy. From 1958/59 incorporates Accounts of Lace furnishings industry (export promotion levy), Wool textile industry (export promotion levy), and Wool textile industry (scientific research levy), previously published separately. Cutlery and stainless steel flatware industry (scientific research levy) added 1965/66. Final payments on Lace industry levies made in 1965/66.
Lace industry

417
Irish Universities Act 1908. Accounts . . . 1909-1920/21.
Supersedes its: Royal University of Ireland. Account . . .
Universities and colleges (Ireland)

418
Iron and Steel Act 1953. Accounts of the transactions of the Iron and Steel Realisation Account . . . 1953/54+.
Iron and steel

419
Iron and Steel (Financial Provisions) Act 1960. Loans to the iron and steel industry (Minister of Power). Account . . . 1960/61+.

420
Isle of Man. Account of revenue and expenditure in respect of the duties of the Customs of the Isle of Man . . . 1866/67-1940/41.
PP: 1866/67-1920/21.
NP: 1921/22-1940/41.
Isle of Man; Man, Isle of

421
Land registry. Accounts of receipts and payments . . . 1883/84-1921/22.
PP: 1883/84-1920/21.
NP: 1921/22.
Land IV.7; IV.5

422
Land Registry (New Buildings) Act 1900. Accounts . . . 1900/1-1915/16.
Land IV.6

423
Legal Aid Acts 1949 to 1964. Legal Aid Fund. Account . . . 1949/50+.
Legal aid

424
Legal Aid (Scotland) Acts 1949-1964.
Legal Aid (Scotland) Fund. Account . . .
1949/50+.
Legal aid (Scotland)

425
Local taxation (Ireland) . . . Account . . .
1899/1906-1919/20.
Local taxation (Ireland)

426
Marshall Aid Commemoration Act 1953.
Marshall Aid Commemoration Commis-
sion. Account . . . 1954/55+.
Marshall Aid Commemoration

427
Ministry of Defence appropriation account . . . 1948/49-1963/64.
From 1964/65, Appropriation accounts for all the fighting Services and
for the Ministry of Defence are combined in its: Defence accounts . . .
Defence

428
Ministry of Food. Appropriation account
. . . 1918/19.
Food IV.1

429
Ministry of Information. Appropriation
account . . . 1918/19.
Information

430
Ministry of Munitions. Appropriation
account . . . 1915/16-1919/20.
Munitions III.2

431
Ministry of Munitions. National and
Royal Aircraft Factories. Annual ac-
counts . . . 1916/17.
No more issued.
Munitions III.5

432
Ministry of Pensions. Appropriation account . . . 1916/17-1918/19.
*Pensions (naval and military
and Air Force) IV.6*

433
Ministry of Shipping. Appropriation ac-
count . . . 1917/18-1919/20.
Shipping III.2

434
National Health Insurance Acts 1936
to 1941 . . . National Health Insurance
Fund. Accounts of the National Health
Insurance Fund (England), the Welsh
National Health Insurance Fund and the
Scottish National Health Insurance Fund
. . . 1912/14-1948.
Originally issued under 1911 Act.
A new National Insurance scheme
came into effect 5 July 1948.
Insurance, National Health IV.11

435
National Land Fund. Account . . . 1946/
47+.
Land IV.15

436
Navy appropriation account . . . 1866/
67-1963/64.
Continues its: Navy. Account of
naval receipt and expenditure . . . 1831/
32-1868/69.
From 1964/65, Appropriation accounts for all the fighting Services are
combined in its: Defence accounts . . .
Navy and marines V.5; Navy IV.2

437
Navy Dockyard and production accounts of shipbuilding and ship repairing in H.M. Dockyards . . . 1867/68-
1963/64.
Title varies: Dockyard expense accounts . . . (to 1933). 1934+ uses revised
form as recommended by Public Accounts Committee for 1935.
From 1964/65 incorporated in its:
Defence accounts . . .
PP: 1867/68-1919/20, 1934-1963/64.
NP: 1920/21-1933.
Not issued: 1914/15-1918/19, 1939/
40-1946/47.
*Dockyards and victualling yards
(naval) IV.13; 3, 5; Navy IV*

438
Public Departments. Gross and net cost.
Statement showing the gross and net
cost of the Civil Services and Revenue
Departments and the Army, Navy and
Air Services . . . 1922/23-1938/39.
Continues statements formerly ap-
pended to the annual Appropriation
accounts.
Revenue and expenditure II.9

439
Public Offices (Acquisition of Site) Act 1895, session 2; Public Offices (Westminster) Site Act 1896; Public Offices (Whitehall) Site Act 1897; Public Buildings Expenses Act 1898 . . . Accounts . . . 1896/97-1921/22.
Offices, public IV.10; III.2

440
Public Offices Site (Dublin) Act 1903. Account . . . 1903/4-1921/22.
Offices, public (Ireland)

441
Redundancy Payments Act 1965. Redundancy Fund. Account . . . 1965/66+.

442
Revenue Departments. Appropriation accounts . . . 1921/22-1961/62.
Continues, in part, its: Civil Services and Revenue Departments. Appropriation accounts . . .
1962/63+, Accounts for Revenue Departments included in Class I of its: Civil appropriation accounts . . .
Civil Service and Revenue Departments IV.3; Appropriation accounts

443
Royal Air Force Prize Fund. Account . . . 1949/50-1958/59.
Air Force IV

444
Royal Naval Prize Fund. Account . . . 1949/50-1955/56.
Navy V

445
Royal Naval Torpedo Factory, Greenock. Annual accounts . . . 1910/11-1913/14.
Navy V.26

446
Royal University of Ireland. Account of receipts and expenditures . . . 1881/82-1909.
Superseded by its: Irish Universities Act 1908. Accounts . . .
Universities and colleges (Ireland)

447
Supreme Court of Judicature (Ireland). Accounts . . . in respect of the funds of suitors . . . 1881/82-1919/20.

Not issued: 1914/15.
Courts of law (Ireland) III.7; III.5

448
Trading accounts and balance sheets of trading or commercial services conducted by government departments . . . 1919/20+.
Finance III.47; Trading accounts

449
Transport Act 1962. Loans to nationalised transport undertakings (Minister of Transport). Account . . . 1963/64+.
Continues its: Finance Act 1956. Transport (Railway Finances) Act 1957. Advances to nationalised industries and undertakings (Minister of Transport). Accounts . . .

450
Uganda Railway Acts 1896 and 1902. Account . . . 1896/97-1906/7.
Uganda II.4; III.5

451
Unemployment insurance. Unemployment Fund account . . . 1912/13-1947/48.
Insurance, National Unemployment IV.16

452
Vote of credit. Expenditure arising out of the war . . . 1938/39-1945/46.
Finance III.50

453
Vote of credit. Expenditure arising out of the war. Appropriation account . . . 1939/40-1945/46.
Finance III.51

454
Vote of credit. Naval and military operations and other expenditure arising out of the war . . . 1914-1918/19.
Some supplementary Votes issued.
Finance III.50

455
Vote of credit (Appropriation Account). Naval and military operations and other expenditure arising out of the war. Appropriation account . . . 1914/15-1920.
Finance III.51

456
Vote of credit. Statement showing the cash transactions . . . 1919/20-1926/27.
Finance III.52

457
War damage account . . . Account prepared pursuant to Section 2(2) of the Miscellaneous Financial Provisions Act 1946 and Sections 2(2), 2(4), and 2(5) of the War Damage Act 1964 . . . 1964/65+.

Replaces its two series, previously issued separately: War damage (business and private chattels scheme). Account . . . ; and: War damage (land and buildings). Account . . .

458
War damage (business and private chattels scheme). Account . . . 1946/47-1963/64.

Preceded by its: War damage (business scheme). Statement . . .; and its: War damage (private chattels scheme). Statement . . .

Superseded by its: War damage account . . . 1964/65+, which replaces this and its: War damage (land and buildings). Account . . .
War damage

459
War damage (business scheme). Statement of the receipts and payments . . . 1941/44-1946.

Superseded by its: War damage (business and private chattels scheme). Account . . .
War damage

460
War damage (land and buildings). Account . . . 1946/47-1963/64.

Superseded by its: War damage account . . . 1964/65+, which replaces this and its: War damage (business and private chattels scheme). Account . . .
War damage

461
War damage (private chattels scheme). Statement of receipts and payments . . . 1941/42-1945/46.

Superseded by its: War damage (business and private chattels scheme). Account . . .
War damage

462
War damage (public utility undertakings). Account . . . 1949/50-1950/51.
War damage

463
War Office purchasing (repayment) services. Appropriation account . . . 1959/60-1963/64.

Later, included in its: Defence accounts . . .

464
Wheat Fund. Accounts . . . 1932/33-1957.
Wheat

465
White Fish and Herring Industries Acts 1953 and 1957 . . . White Fish Authority. Account . . . 1953/54+.
Fisheries IV

466
Widows', Orphans' and Old Age Contributory Pensions Acts . . . Accounts . . . 1926/27-1947/48.
Pensions (contributory and old age) IV.15

Fishery Board for Scotland

Set up by 1882 Act, replacing the Commissioners for the British White Herring Fisheries.

467
North Sea fishery investigation. Northern area. Report . . . 1-5, 1902/3-1908/11.

For Report on Southern area, see: Marine Biological Association of the United Kingdom.

See also: Delegates to International Hydrographic Conferences.
Fisheries III.10

Foreign and Commonwealth Office

Formed in 1968 by the merging of the *Foreign Office and the *Commonwealth Office.

468

Colonial Development and Welfare Act. Return of schemes made and of loans approved under the Act . . . 1942/43+.

Issued by Colonial Office, 1942/43-1964/65; by Commonwealth Office, 1965/66-1966/67.

Colonies III.5; IV

469

Miscellaneous papers . . . 1875+.
Numbered serially each session.
Miscellaneous papers

470

Treaties, etc., with foreign states. . . . Supplementary list of ratifications, accessions, withdrawals . . . 1922+.

Title varies: . . . Supplementary list . . . 1934+.

Earlier, see: Foreign Office. Accessions . . . of foreign states to various international treaty engagements.
Treaties II.1

471

Treaty series . . . 1892+.
Numbered serially each year.
Treaties

472

Treaty series. General index . . . 1892/96+.
Treaties III.1; IV

473

Treaty series. Index . . . [annual] 1910+.
1943-1946 covered by a single index.
Treaties IV

Foreign Compensation Commission

Established by the Foreign Compensation Act 1950 to register, determine, and distribute claims against foreign governments, following agreements of 1948 and 1949 with the governments of Jugoslavia and Czechoslovakia for compensation by them in respect of British property rights.

474

Annual report . . . 1, 1950/51+.
In Foreign and Commonwealth Office. Miscellaneous papers.
Foreign compensation

Foreign Office

Resulted from the reallocation of duties of the two Secretaries of State in 1782, one becoming responsible for home affairs and the other for foreign affairs. In 1968 the Foreign Office was merged with the *Commonwealth Office to form the *Foreign and Commonwealth Office.

475

Accessions . . . of foreign states to various international treaty engagements . . . 1908-1919.

Later, see Foreign and Commonwealth Office. Treaties, etc., with foreign states. . . . Supplementary list of ratifications, accessions, withdrawals . . .
Treaties II.1

476

Accessions to and withdrawals from various treaty engagements between the United Kingdom and foreign powers . . . 1907-1911.

Lists accessions and withdrawals of British colonies.
Treaties II.1

477

Churchill Endowment Fund for the exchange of students between Great Britain and Denmark. Accounts and statements of scholarships awarded . . . 1953/56-1964/67.

478

Council of Europe. Committee of Ministers. Report on the proceedings . . . 2nd-7th sessions, 1949-1951.

In Foreign and Commonwealth Office. Miscellaneous papers.

Reports on 1st, 4th, 8th+ not issued. A brief report of the 1st session is included in its: Council of Europe. Report on the proceedings . . . 1st session. (1948/49 Cmd. 7807)
Council of Europe

479

Council of Europe. Consultative Assembly. Report on the proceedings . . . 2nd-9th sessions, 1950-1957/58.

In Foreign and Commonwealth Office. Miscellaneous papers.

Reports on 1st, 10th+ not issued. A brief report of the 1st session is included in its: Council of Europe. Report on the proceedings ... 1st session. (1948/49 Cmd. 7807)

Council of Europe

480
Diplomatic and consular reports. Annual series. 1-5566, 1886-1916.

1-2033, 1886-1898, as Diplomatic and consular reports on trade and finance.

Not printed: nos. 5511, 5527, 5549, 5550 (1914/16 session).

See also: Board of Trade. Commercial reports ...

Trade III.4; III.23

481
Diplomatic and consular reports. Miscellaneous series. 1-687, 1886-1914.

1-450, 1886-March 1888, as Reports on subjects of general and commercial interest.

Later reports listed as: Commercial reports (Miscellaneous series).

See also: Board of Trade. Commercial reports ...

Trade III.4; III.23

482
Economic cooperation. Report on operations under the Economic Cooperation Agreement between the governments of the United Kingdom and the United States of America ... 1-18, 1949-1954.

Treaties I. United States 32; United States II

483
Egypt. Reports by H.M. Agent and Consul-General on the finances, administration, and condition of Egypt and the Soudan ... 1889-1920.

A single Report was issued for 1914/19.

Egypt 25; I.1

484
European Coal and Steel Community. Annual report of the Council of Association between the Government of the United Kingdom ... and the High Authority of the European Coal and Steel Community. 1, 1955/56+.

In Foreign and Commonwealth Office. Miscellaneous papers.

Treaties

485
Foreign Compensation Act 1950. Foreign Compensation Commission accounts ... 1950/51+.

Title varies: Accounts of the Yugoslav and Czechoslovak Funds ...

Foreign compensation

486
Index to consular reports. Index to reports of ... diplomatic and consular representatives abroad on trade and subjects of general interest. (With Appendix). 1886/88-1914.

Trade III.4; III.23

487
Joint Export-Import Agency. Report of Price, Waterhouse & Co. on the accounts ... 1947/48-1949.

Agency established January 1947 to deal with foreign trade of the combined United Kingdom and United States zones in Germany. The Government of the Federal Republic assumed responsibility in October 1949.

Germany II

488
Mombasa-Victoria (Uganda) Railway. Report ... on the progress of the works ... 1896/97-1903/4.

Uganda

489
Report on the proceedings ... of the General Assembly of the United Nations. 2nd session, 1947+.

Treaties III.7; United Nations

490
Sudan. Report ... 1921-1951/52.

Reports for 1939/41 and 1942/44 issued in 1950/51.

Sudan

491
Suez Canal. Annual return of shipping and tonnage ... 1869/82-1953/55.

PP: 1869/82-1920.
NP: 1921-1953/55.
Not issued: 1940-1944.

Suez Canal

492
United Nations. Disarmament Commission. Report on the proceedings of the Sub-Committee ... 1954-1957.

United Nations

493

United Nations. Disarmament Commission. Verbatim records of the meetings ... of the Sub-Committee ... 1st-68th meetings, 1954-1955.

United Nations

494

United Nations Relief and Rehabilitation Administration. Resolutions adopted by the Council ... 1st-6th sessions, 1943-1947.

In Foreign and Commonwealth Office. Miscellaneous papers.

Treaties III.22

Forestry Commission

Established by Forestry Act 1919; lapsed on outbreak of war in 1939 and was reconstituted by Forestry Act 1945.

495

Annual report of the Forestry Commissioners ... 1, 1919/20+.

Not issued: 20-25, 1938/39-1943/44.

Forestry

Furniture and Timber Industry Training Board

Established December 1965 under Industrial Training Act 1964.

496

Report and statement of accounts ... 1965/66+.

Gas Council

Established May 1949 under the Gas Act 1948, with responsibility for Area Gas Boards.

497

Annual report and accounts ... 1, 1948/50+.

Gas

Gas Industry Training Board

Established June 1965 under Industrial Training Act 1964.

498

Report and statement of accounts ... 1965/66+.

General Board of Commissioners in Lunacy for Scotland

The Commissioners were appointed under the Lunatics (Scotland) Act 1857 and were replaced in 1914 by the *General Board of Control for Scotland.

499

Annual report ... 1-56, 1858-1914.

Superseded by: General Board of Control for Scotland. Annual report ...

Lunacy (Scotland)

General Board of Control for Scotland

Set up May 1914 under the Mental Deficiency and Lunacy (Scotland) Act 1913, assuming the powers of the *General Board of Commissioners in Lunacy for Scotland. The Board was dissolved June 1962 under the Mental Health (Scotland) Act 1960, being replaced by the Mental Welfare Commission for Scotland.

500

Annual report ... 1914-1961.

Title varies: Annual report (Lunacy and mental deficiency).

Supersedes: General Board of Commissioners in Lunacy for Scotland. Annual report ...

From 1947-1953 the Board furnished information on mental health, included in: Department of Health for Scotland. Annual report.

Not issued: 1939/40-1953.

Lunacy (Scotland);
Mental health (Scotland)

General Practice Finance Corporation

Corporation established November 1966, to make loans to medical practitioners to encourage the development of premises for general practice.

501
National Health Service Act 1966. Report of the General Practice Finance Corporation . . . 1, 1966/67+.

General Register Office

Established by the Births and Deaths Registration Act 1836.

502
Annual report . . . of births, deaths and marriages in England and Wales . . . 1-83, 1837-1920.
 Continued by its: Registrar-General's statistical review of England and Wales. (NP) 1921+.
 PP: 1-82, 1837-1919.
 NP: 83, 1920.
Births, etc.

503
Annual report . . . of births, deaths and marriages in England and Wales. Decennial supplement . . . 1851/60-1901/10.
 Continued by its: Registrar-General's Decennial supplement. 1921+. (NP) (Not issued for 1941)
Births, etc.

504
Census of England and Wales. 1861+.
 Earlier censuses: 1801-1841 of Great Britain; 1851 of England, Wales, and Scotland. (All in PP)
 PP: 1861-1911; 1921 Preliminary report.
 NP: 1921+.
 No census was taken in 1941.
Population

505
General abstract of marriages, births, and deaths registered in England and Wales . . . 1857/58-1914.
Births, etc.

General Register Office, Scotland

Established by the Scottish Registration Act 1855.

506
Annual report of the Registrar-General for Scotland on the births, deaths and marriages registered in Scotland . . . 1, 1855+.
 1864-1917 includes: Vaccination in Scotland. Annual report . . . 1-54.
 PP: 1-64, 1855-1919.
 NP: 65, 1920+.
Births, etc. (Scotland)

507
Census of Scotland. 1861+.
 Earlier censuses in PP: 1801-1841 of Great Britain; 1851 of England, Wales, and Scotland.
 PP: 1861-1911.
 NP: 1921+.
 No census was taken in 1941.
Population (Scotland)

508
Detailed annual report of the Registrar-General of births, deaths and marriages in Scotland . . . 1-58, 1859-1912.
 From 1913, Annual report of the Registrar-General for Scotland is expanded to include much of the detailed information contained in these reports.
Births, etc. (Scotland)

509
Vaccination in Scotland. Annual report . . . 1-54, 1864-1917.
 In its: Annual report of the Registrar-General for Scotland on the births, deaths and marriages registered in Scotland . . . 11-64, 1865-1917.
Vaccination (Scotland)

Glasgow. University

510
Annual report on the state of the finances . . . 1889/90-1913/14.
 Title varies: Abstract of accounts . . .
Universities and colleges (Scotland)

511
Annual statistical report . . . 1898/99-

1913/14.
Universities and colleges (Scotland)

Government Actuary

The Government Actuary's Department was set up by Treasury Minute in July 1918.

512
Education (Scotland) Acts . . . Report by the Government Actuary on the Teachers Superannuation Scheme (Scotland) . . . 1, 1933+.

Intended to be septennial, following 1925 Act, but war affected regularity; 2nd report, published 1951, covers to 1948.
Education and schools (Scotland) III.13

513
House of Commons Members' Fund. Report of the Government Actuary . . . 1944+.

Fund established October 1939. Reports are quinquennial.
House of Commons

514
National Insurance Acts . . . Interim report by the Government Actuary . . . 1948/50+.

Note also its: National Insurance Acts 1946 to 1964. Report . . . on the quinquennial review . . .
Insurance, National III

515
National Insurance Acts 1946 to 1964. Report by the Government Actuary on the quinquennial review . . . 1, 1948/54+.

Note also its: National Insurance Acts . . . Interim report . . .
Insurance, National III

516
National Insurance (Industrial Injuries) Acts . . . Interim report by the Government Actuary . . . 1948/50+.

Note also its: National Insurance (Industrial Injuries) Acts 1946 to 1964. Report . . . on the quinquennial review . . .
Insurance, National (industrial injuries) III

517
National Insurance (Industrial Injuries) Acts 1946 to 1964. Report by the Government Actuary on the quinquennial review . . . 1, 1948/54+.

Note also its: National Insurance (Industrial Injuries) Acts . . . Interim report . . .
Insurance, National (industrial injuries) III

518
Teachers (Superannuation) Act 1925. Report by the Government Actuary on the "1926 Scheme" relating to teachers in contributory service in schools which are not grant-aided . . . 1, 1933+.

Intended to be septennial, but war affected regularity; 2nd Report, published 1951, covers to 1948.
Education and schools III.38

519
Teachers (Superannuation) Acts. Report by the Government Actuary on the Teachers Superannuation Scheme (England and Wales) . . . 1, 1933+.

Intended to be septennial, following 1925 Act, but war affected regularity; 2nd Report, published 1951, covers 1933/48.
Education and schools III.38

520
Unemployment Insurance Bill . . . Report by the Government Actuary on the financial provisions of the Bill . . . 1919-1929.
Insurance, National Unemployment IV.17

Greenwich. Royal Observatory

521
Report of the Astronomer Royal to the Board of Visitors of the Royal Observatory, Greenwich . . . 1879; 1896/97-1914/15.
Greenwich Observatory

Harwich Harbour Conservancy Board

522
Abstract of the accounts . . . 1863/66-

1906/7.
    Title varies: Accounts . . . 1863/66-
1878/79.
Harwich Harbour

Herring Industry Board

Set up in 1935 under the Herring
Industry Act. Most of its functions were
suspended from November 1939 to
January 1945.

523
Annual report. 1, 1935/36+.
    PP: 3, 1937/38+.
    NP: 1-2, 1935/36-1936/37.
    Not issued: 4-10, 1938/39-1944/45.
Fisheries III

Highlands and Islands Medical Service Board

524
Report . . . 1-5, 1914-1918.
Highlands and Islands

Historic Buildings Council for England

Appointed October 1953 under Historic
Buildings and Ancient Monuments Act
1953.

525
Annual report . . . 1, 1953+.
*Historic buildings
and ancient monuments*

Historic Buildings Council for Scotland

Appointed October 1953 under Historic
Buildings and Ancient Monuments Act
1953.

526
Annual report . . . 1, 1953+.
*Historic buildings
and ancient monuments*

Historic Buildings Council for Wales

Appointed October 1953 under Historic
Buildings and Ancient Monuments Act
1953.

527
Annual report . . . 1, 1953+.
*Historic buildings
and ancient monuments*

Home Grown Cereals Authority

Established in June 1965 by the Cereals
Marketing Act, to improve the marketing of homegrown cereals.

528
Annual report and accounts . . . 1, 1965/
66+.

Home Office

Evolved from the reallocation of duties
of the two Secretaries of State in 1782,
one becoming responsible for foreign
affairs, the other for home and, until
1801, colonial affairs. Its range of functions is very wide, since it is responsible
for all domestic matters not assigned by
law or custom to some other agency.
Particularly important are matters relating to public safety and to aliens.

529
Agriculture Acts 1947 and 1957. Annual review and determination of guarantees . . . 1951+.
    Title varies: 1951-1953, Annual re-
view and fixing of farm prices . . .
    Issued jointly by Home Office, Min-
istry of Agriculture, Fisheries and Food,
and Secretary of State for Scotland.
Agriculture IV

530
Aliens Act 1905. Annual report of
H.M. Inspector . . . with a statement as

to the expulsion of aliens . . . 1-9, 1906-1914.

Aliens III.2

531
Aliens Act 1905. Return of alien passengers brought to the United Kingdom from ports in Europe or within the Mediterranean Sea . . . with the number of expulsion orders . . . 1906-April/June 1914.

Quarterly, but gives monthly figures for each port.

Continues: Board of Trade. Alien immigration . . .

Continued by: Home Office. Aliens Order 1920. Return of aliens landed, embarked and refused leave to land in the United Kingdom . . . 1920+.

Aliens IV.2

532
Aliens (naturalisation). Return showing particulars of all aliens . . . to whom certificates of naturalisation have been issued . . . 1854/68-1961.

Early issues irregular.

Naturalisation

533
Aliens Order 1920. Return of aliens landed, embarked, and refused leave to land in the United Kingdom. 1920-1938/39.

Continues its: Aliens Act 1905. Return of alien passengers brought to the United Kingdom from ports in Europe . . .

Aliens IV.2

534
Benefices Act 1898. Return of transfers of rights of patronage . . . 1899-1904/12.

Benefices

535
Betting, Gaming and Lotteries Act 1963. Permits and licences. 1960/61+.

Until 1962: Betting and Gaming Act 1960. Permits and licences.

536
Cases of industrial poisoning and fatal accidents in factories and workshops. Preliminary tables . . . 1906-1913.

Published in advance of, and also incorporated in: Factory Inspectors' Office. Factories and workshops. Annual report . . . (This is now: Department of Employment and Productivity. Factory Inspectorate. Annual report of H.M. Chief Inspector of Factories . . .)

Factories

537
Children in care in England and Wales. Particulars of the number of children in the care of local authorities under the Children Act 1948 . . . 1952+.

Children and young persons

538
Commonwealth Immigrants Act 1962. Control of immigration. Statistics . . . 1962/63+.

Presented jointly with Ministry of Labour.

539
Continuance of emergency legislation. Memorandum . . . 1950-1957.

Laws, emergency

540
Corporal punishment (sentences). Return of all sentences of corporal punishment . . . 1876/94-1909.

Corporal punishment

541
Criminal statistics, England and Wales . . . 1922+.

Continues, in part, its: Judicial statistics . . .

1939/45 covered by single summary report.

Judicial statistics; Criminal statistics

542
Deaths from starvation, or accelerated by privation (London). Return . . . 1868/70-1907.

Title varies: Starvation (metropolis). Return . . .

Continued in: Local Government Board. Deaths from starvation, or accelerated by privation (England and Wales).

Starvation

543
Election expenses. Return . . . 1834+.

Title varies: Parliamentary elections. . .

Elections I.2; IV.14; IV.7

544
Emergency Powers (Defence) Act 1939.
Defence Regulation 18B. Reports by
the Secretary of State as to the action
taken under Regulation 18B of the
Defence (General) Regulations 1939 . . .
Sept./Nov. 1939-April 1945.
Emergency powers

545
Experiments on living animals . . . Re-
turn . . . 1, 1878+.
Vivisection; Animals

546
Judicial statistics. 1856-1921.
1856 in three parts: 1. Police and
constabulary; 2. Criminal proceedings;
3. Prisons.
1857-1921 in two parts: 1. Criminal;
2. Civil.
Continued 1922+ in two separate
publications: Home Office. Criminal sta-
tistics, England and Wales . . . ; and: Lord
Chancellor's Office. Judicial statistics,
England and Wales . . . Civil . . .
PP: 1878-1914, Pt. 1; 1917-1919.
NP: 1914, Pt. 2-1916; 1920-1921.
Statistical tables III.11;
Judicial statistics

547
Lead poisoning. Return giving the number of cases of lead poisoning reported
in the manufacture of earthenware and
china . . . distinguishing the processes,
and showing the number of workers
suspended . . . 1899/1900 (Jan.-May)-
1900.
Lead

548
Lead poisoning. Return of the number
of cases of lead poisoning reported as
occurring in the earthenware and china
industry, for each month . . . Jan. 1898/
March 1900-Jan. 1898/Dec. 1900.
Lead

549
Lead poisoning. Return showing, with
reference to the cases of lead poisoning
reported . . . in the earthenware and
china industry, the severity of the at-
tack, the number of previous attacks,
and the main symptoms referable to
lead poisoning. 1899/1900-1899/1904.
Lead

550
Licensing statistics. Statistics as to the
operation and administration of the
laws relating to the sale of intoxicating
liquor . . . 1905-1938.
Licensing acts IV.11

551
Members of Parliament. Return . . .
1880/85-1924/29.
Continues its: Return of the name of
every Member of the Lower House of
Parliament . . . from 1213 to 1874.
[1878 (69-I) 1xii]
House of Commons; Parliament

552
Offences of drunkenness. Statistics of
the number of offences of drunkenness
proved in England and Wales . . . 1950+.
Drunkenness

553
Offences relating to motor vehicles.
Return . . . 1928+.
Title varies: 1928-1938/39, Motoring
offences. Return . . .
Not issued: 1939/40-1945.
Motor vehicles

554
Parliamentary constituencies (electors,
etc.) (United Kingdom). Return . . .
1873-1919.
Elections IV.13; IV.15

555
Probation of first offenders. Return . . .
1888/90-1903/5.
First offenders;
Probation of offenders

556
Prosecution of Offences Acts 1879,
1884, and 1908. Return showing the
working of the regulations . . . with statistics . . . setting forth the number, nature, cost, and results of the proceedings
. . . 1880/83-1914.
Prosecutions, public

557
Report of H.M. Chief Inspector of
Constabulary . . . 1856/57+.
Title varies. To 1962: Police, coun-
ties and boroughs, England and Wales.
Reports of H.M. Inspectors of Con-
stabulary . . .

Not issued: 1939/40-1943/44. Report for 1944/45 reviews these years.
Police

558
State management districts. (Licensing Act 1964 and Licensing (Scotland) Act 1959). Annual report . . . 1, 1921/22+.
Supersedes: Central Control Board (Liquor Traffic). Defence of the Realm (Liquor Control) Regulations 1915. General manager's report on the Carlisle and District Direct Control Area . . .
Originally issued in pursuance of Licensing Act 1921.
Title varies: 1921/22-1927/28, State management districts. General manager's report . . .
Licensing acts III.5

559
Statistics of foreigners entering and leaving the United Kingdom. 1921+.
Title varies: 1921-1938, Aliens Restriction Acts 1914 and 1919. Aliens Order 1920. Statistics in regard to alien passengers who entered and left the United Kingdom.
1939/51 covered by single report.
Aliens IV.2

560
Statistics of persons acquiring citizenship of the United Kingdom and colonies. 1962+.

561
Statistics relating to approved schools, remand homes and attendance centres in England and Wales . . . 1961+.

562
Sunday Entertainments Act 1932. Cinematograph Fund. Account . . . 1933/34+.
Cinematographs

563
Workmen's compensation. Statistics of proceedings under the Workmen's Compensation Acts and the Employer's Liability Act 1880 . . . 1898-1938.
Not issued: 1915-1918.
Employer's liability III.2; Workmen's compensation IV.6

Home Office. Children's Department

564
Report on the work of the Children's Department . . . 1-8, 1923-1955/60; n.s., 1, 1961/63+.
Supersedes: Inspector of Reformatory and Industrial Schools. Report.
1-5, 1923-1938 as: Home Office. Children's Branch. Report . . .
PP: n.s., 1, 1961/63+.
NP: 1-8, 1923-1955/60.

Home Office. Explosions in Mines Committee

565
Report . . . 1-7, 1912-1915.
Explosions III.5

Home Office. Fire Service Department

566
Fire services. Report of H.M. Chief Inspector of Fire Services (counties and county boroughs, England and Wales) . . . 1948+.
Fire

Home Office. Prison Department

567
Prisons and Borstals . . . Report on the work of the Prison Department. 1963+.
Supersedes: Prison Commission. Prisons . . .
Issued in two volumes, the second containing statistical tables.

Home Office. Probation and After-Care Department

568
Report on the work of the . . . Department. 1, 1962/65+.

**Hotel and Catering Industry
Training Board**

Established November 1966 under Industrial Training Act 1964.

569
Report and statement of accounts . . .
·1966/67+.

Housing Corporation

Established under the Housing Act 1964,
to promote and assist in the development of Housing Societies.

570
Housing Act 1964. Report of the Housing Corporation. 1, 1964/65+.

Hydrographic Office

571
Report on Admiralty surveys. 1879-
1932.
    1925-1932, in its: Catalogue of charts,
etc. . . . (NP).
    PP: 1879-1913.
    NP: 1920-1921, 1925-1932.
    Not issued: 1914-1919; 1922-1924.
            Surveys III.1; Navy III.6

**Imperial Conference of Prime Ministers
and Representatives of the United
Kingdom, the Dominions and India**

572
Summary of proceedings and appendices.
1911-1937.
    Irregular.
    Later, see: Commonwealth Office.
Commonwealth Prime Ministers' meeting. Final communiqué. 1962+.
            Imperial conferences

Imperial Economic Committee

573
Report . . . on marketing and preparing

for market of foodstuffs produced in
the overseas parts of the Empire. 1925-
1940/47.
    PP: 1925-1928.
    NP: 1929-1940/47.
            Imperial Economic Committee

Imperial Entomological Conference

574
Report on the Imperial Entomological
Conference . . . 1-2, 1920-1925.
    Later reports published by Common-
wealth Institute of Entomology (with
title changed to Commonwealth Entomological Conference), not issued as
government publications.
            Entomological research

Imperial Institute, London

Established 1887 to give scientific and
technical advice in the interests of the
economic development of the natural
resources of the Empire.

575
Annual report . . . 1891/92-1914.
    Later reports not issued as govern-
ment publications.
    1902-1905 Reports are to Board of
Trade; 1906/07-1914 Reports are in
Colonial Office Annual series.
    PP: 1905-1914.
    NP: 1891/92-1904.
            Imperial Institute

576
Northern Nigeria. Report on the results
of the mineral survey . . . 1-5, 1904/5-
1907/9.
    In Colonial Office. Colonial reports
. . . Miscellaneous.
            Nigeria

577
Nyasaland. Report on the results of the
mineral survey . . . 1-3, 1906/7-1908/9.
    In Colonial Office. Colonial reports
. . . Miscellaneous.
            Nyasaland

578
Southern Nigeria. Report on the results
of the mineral survey . . . 1903/5-1913.

In Colonial Office. Colonial reports
... Miscellaneous.

Nigeria

Imperial Institute, London.
Indian Section

579
Annual report ... 1899/1900-1906/7.
Imperial Institute

Imperial Shipping Committee

580
Report on the work of the Imperial
Shipping Committee ... 1920/22-
1933/36.
PP: 1920/22-1930/32.
NP: 1933/36.
Shipping II.1 (g)

581
Reports ... 1921-1938.
Irregular reports on various subjects.
PP: 1921-1933.
NP: 1934-1938.
Shipping II.1

Imperial War Museum

582
Report ... 1-21, 1917/18-1938/39.
PP: 1-4, 1917/18-1920/21.
NP: 5-21, 1921/22-1938/39.
Imperial War Museum

Independent Television Authority

Established by Television Act 1954.

583
Annual report and accounts ... 1,
1954/55+.
Broadcasting

India Office

The Office was set up in 1858 to replace
the administration of India by the East
India Company, after the mutiny of
1857. The Office was abolished in 1947,
following the Indian Independence Act,
and relations with India and Pakistan
became the responsibility of the Commonwealth Relations Office.

584
East India (accounts and estimates).
Explanatory memorandum by the Under
Secretary of State for India. 1887/88-
1936/37.
East India 60; IV.1

585
East India (annual estimates). Estimate
of revenue and expenditure ... com-
pared with results of previous years ...
1883/84-1936/37.
PP: 1883/84-1920/21.
NP: 1921/22-1936/37.
Not issued: 1916/17-1919/20.
East India 60; IV.1

586
East India (budget). Return of the bud-
get of the Governor General of India in
Council ... 1879/80-1939/40.
Title varies: 1879/80-1921/22, East
India (financial statement and budget).
Return ...
PP: 1879/80-1921/22, 1923/24-1939/
40.
NP: 1922/23.
East India 66: IV.47

587
East India (education). Progress of edu-
cation in India. Quinquennial review.
1-9, 1881/85-1922/27.
PP: 3-7, 1892/97-1912/17.
NP: 1-2, 1881/85-1887/92; 8-9, 1917/
22-1922/27.
East India 59; IV.38

588
East India (elections). Return showing
the results of elections. 1920-1937.
East India IV.39

589
East India (home accounts). Home ac-
counts of the government of India.
1852/53-1936/37.
Preceded by: East India Company.
Home accounts. 1834/35-1851/52.
PP: 1852/53-1919/20.
NP: 1920/21-1936/37.
East India 81; IV.54

590
East India (income and expenditure).
Return . . . 1861/78-1917/20.
East India 149; IV.57

591
East India (India Store Department).
Return of the report on the work of
the India Store Department. 1922/23-
1926/27.
PP: 1924/25.
NP: 1922/23-1923/24, 1925/26-1926/
27.
East India IV.109

592
East India (loans raised in England).
Return . . . 1873-1940.
PP: 1873-1921.
NP: 1921/22-1940.
East India 106; IV.67

593
East India (loans raised in India). Return of all loans chargeable on the
revenues of India. April/Sept. 1873-
1917/18.
East India 106; IV.68

594
East India (progress and conditions).
Statement . . . 1-70, 1859/60-1934/35.
1891/92, 1901/2, 1911/12, include
3rd-5th Decennial Reports.
Not issued: 1862/63-1863/64.
East India 141; IV.87

595
East India (railways). Administration report on the railways in India. 1859-
1913/14.
Later reports issued by: India. Railway Board.
East India 145; III.35

596
East India (railways and irrigation works).
Return . . . 1900/1-1915/16.
East India IV.94

597
East India (sanitary measures). Report
. . . 1-49, 1869-1915/16.
Title varies.
PP: 8-49, 1874/75-1915/16.
NP: 1-7, 1869-1873/74.
East India 154; III.44

598
East India (statistical abstract). Statis-
tical abstract for British India . . . 1-72,
1840/65-1930/40.
Statistical tables III.10;
East India IV.107

599
East India (trade). Review of the trade
of India. 1895/96-1918/19.
Later continued under: India. Com-
mercial Intelligence Department.
East India 176; IV.114

600
East India (trade). Tables relating to the
trade of British India with British possessions and foreign countries, for the
five years . . . 1893/98-1913/18.
Continues its: East India (trade).
Statement of the trade of British India
. . . 1869/74-1892/97.
East India 176; IV.114

Indian Students' Department

601
Report . . . 1912/13-1921/22.
Continued by: India. High Commis-
sioner in London. Education Depart-
ment. Report . . .
PP: 1912/13-1915/16.
NP: 1920/21-1921/22.
Not issued: 1916/17-1919/20.
East India III.49

Industrial Coal Consumers Council

602
Reports of the Industrial Coal Con-
sumers Council and the Domestic Coal
Consumers Council . . . 1, 1947/48+.
Presented pursuant to Coal Industry
Nationalisation Act 1946.
Coal III.7

Industrial Reorganisation Corporation

Established in 1966 to promote the
greater efficiency and competitiveness
of British industry.

603
Report and accounts . . . 1, 1966/68+.

Inland Revenue Department

Formed by the consolidation of the Board of Excise and the Board of Stamps and Taxes into the Board of Commissioners of Inland Revenue, under the Inland Revenue Board Act 1849. In 1909, responsibility for excise business was transferred to the new *Customs and Excise.

604
Brewers' licences. Return . . . 1851/52-1913/14.
Beer

605
Income tax assessments. Return . . . 1857/59-1903/5.
Title and frequency vary.
Income tax

606
Report of the Commissioners of H.M. Inland Revenue . . . 1855/56+.
Inland revenue

Inspector for Scotland under the Inebriates Acts

607
Report . . . 1-13, 1903-1918.
PP: 1-11, 1903-1914/15.
NP: 12-13, 1916/17-1918.
Drunkards and drunkenness (Scotland)

Inspector of Ancient Monuments

608
Report . . . 1910/11-1912/13.
Historical monuments

Inspector of Reformatory and Industrial Schools

609
Report . . . 1-59, 1857/58-1915.

Superseded by: Home Office. Children's Department. Report . . . 1923+.
Reformatory and industrial schools; Reformatories

Inspector under the Inebriates Acts

610
Report . . . 1-34, 1880-1913.
1880-1907 as: Inspector of Retreats for Inebriates. Report . . .
Drunkards and drunkenness

Inspectors of Explosives

611
Explosives Acts 1875 and 1923. Report of H.M. Inspectors of Explosives . . . 1, 1875+.
Explosives; Explosions

Inter-Departmental Committee on Prices of Building Materials

612
Chairman's report . . . 1923-1933.
Irregular.
Building

613
Interim report . . . 1-6, 1923-1934.
Building

International Commission for Supervision and Control in Laos

614
Interim report . . . 1-4, 1954-1957/58.
Laos

International Commission for Supervision and Control in Vietnam

615
Interim report . . . 1-11, 1954-1960/61.
Vietnam

International Conference on the Sleeping Sickness

616
Proceedings . . . 1, 1908.
 In Foreign and Colonial Office. Miscellaneous papers.
 Proceedings of 2nd Conference, 1928, not issued as British government publication.
Sleeping sickness

International Labour Conference

617
Recommendations . . . adopted by the International Labour Conference at its . . . session. 1-25, 1919-1939.
 Title varies: Draft conventions and recommendations . . .
Treaties II.91

International Sugar Commission

618
Findings of the Permanent Commission . . . 1903-1905.
 Includes Report of the British delegate, later published separately.
Sugar

619
Report of the British delegate . . . 1905-1912.
 Earlier reports in: International Sugar Commission. Findings of the Permanent Commission . . . 1903-1905.
 The United Kingdom withdrew from the Sugar Convention in 1913.
Sugar

Iron and Steel Board

Established under Iron and Steel Act 1953 to exercise general supervision of the industry.

620
Annual report . . . 1, 1953/54+.
Iron and steel

Iron and Steel Consumers' Council

Council appointed July 1951; dissolved July 1953 under Iron and Steel Act 1953.

621
Report . . . 1-2, 1952-1953.
Iron and steel

Iron and Steel Corporation

Appointed October 1950, under the Iron and Steel Act 1949, to administer nationalized companies. Dissolved by the Iron and Steel Act 1953, which returned the companies to private ownership.

622
Report and statement of accounts . . . 1-2, 1950/51-1951/52.
Iron and steel

Iron and Steel Holding and Realisation Agency

Established under the Iron and Steel Act 1953, the Agency superseded the *Iron and Steel Corporation, its principal task being to return companies to private ownership. The Agency was dissolved in 1967.

623
Report and statement of accounts . . . 1953/54-1966/67.
Iron and steel

Iron and Steel Industry Training Board

Established July 1964 under Industrial Training Act 1964.

624
Report and statement of accounts . . . 1964/65+.

Knitting, Lace and Net Industry Training Board

Established March 1966 under Industrial Training Act 1964.

625
Report and statement of accounts . . . 1966+.

Laboratory of the Government Chemist

A separate Laboratory for the Government Chemist was first established in 1897. His principal duties are the inspection of food and drugs for adulteration, mostly in the investigation of cases under the Sale of Food and Drugs Acts.

626
Report of the Government Chemist . . . 1896/97+.
   Agency title varies: Government Laboratory, 1896/97-1909/10; Department of the Government Chemist, 1910/11-1960.
   PP: 1896/97-1920/21.
   NP: 1921/22+.
   Not issued: 1939/40-1948/49.
Laboratories; Government Laboratory

Land Commission

Appointed in February 1967, under the Land Commission Act 1967, to acquire and dispose of land for development and to collect a levy on the development value realized in land transactions.

627
Report and accounts . . . 1, 1967/68+.
   Presented under Land Commission Act 1967.

Land Purchase Commission, Northern Ireland

628
Accounts . . . 1923/24-1936/37.

Continued by: Supreme Court of Judicature, Northern Ireland. Land purchase. Account . . . 1937/38+.
Land, etc. (Ireland) IV.1

Land Registry

629
Report of the Chief Registrar. 1899/1901+.
   PP: 1899/1901-1919.
   NP: 1920/21+.
   Not issued: 1905/6-1911/12, 1922/23-1925/26.
Land, etc. III.4

630
Return showing the work done . . . under the Land Transfer Acts 1875 and 1897, the Small Holdings Act 1892, the Land Registry Act 1862, etc. . . . 1882/94-1912/14.
Land, etc. IV.7

Law Commission

Set up by the Law Commissions Act 1965 in order to promote reform of the law.

631
Annual report . . . 1, 1965/66+.
   PP: 3, 1967/68+.
   NP: 1-2, 1965/66-1966/67.

631a
Law Com. no. 1, 1965+.
   Reports on various subjects related to law reform including the Commission's Annual reports.
   PP: 6, 8, 11A, 15+.
   NP: 1-5, 7, 9-11, 12-14.

Law Reform Committee

Appointed in June 1952, to consider legal problems referred by the Lord Chancellor and to report on the desirability of changes in the existing law.

632
Report . . . 1, 1953+.

Law

Law Reform Committee (Scotland)

Appointed in December 1954, to review and report on changes that might
be desirable in the Scottish law.

633
Report . . . 1, 1957+.

Law (Scotland)

Local Government Board

Established by the Local Government
Act 1871, replacing the Poor Law Board
and assuming powers relating to the
registration of births, public health, and
taxation previously exercised by the
Home Office and the Board of Trade. It
was dissolved in 1919, all its powers
being transferred to the *Ministry of
Health.

634
Annual report . . . 1-48, 1871-1918/19.

Local government

635
Annual report of the Chief Medical
Officer. 1-13, 1858-1870; series 2, 1-8,
1873-1875; series 3, 1-48, 1876-1918/19.
Title varies.
Series 2, 1873-1875, includes three
annual and five supplementary reports.
Continued by: Ministry of Health.
On the state of the public health . . .

*Health, public III.1;
Local government III.2*

636
Deaths from starvation, or accelerated
by privation (England and Wales). 1908-
1918.
Earlier, see: Home Office. Deaths
from starvation, or accelerated by privation (London). Return . . .

Starvation

637
Housing and town planning. Memorandum . . . relative to the operation of
the Housing, Town Planning, etc. Act
1909 . . . 1-4, 1910-1913.

Housing IV.15

638
Local taxation account. Return . . . showing the distribution of the proceeds of
the local taxation licences . . . Account
. . . 1889/90-1908/9.

Local taxation IV.7; II.4, 5

639
Local taxation licences. Return of the
amount received in respect of each
administrative county and county bor-
ough in England and Wales . . . 1889/90-
1909/10.

Local taxation IV.7; II.6

640
London (Equalisation of Rates) Act
1894 . . . Return . . . 1894/95-1913/14.

London IV.16; IV.17

641
Metropolitan water companies (accounts).
Return of the metropolitan water com-
panies . . . 1871-1902.

Water supply IV.3; London IV.19

642
Pauperism (England and Wales). Monthly comparative return of paupers relieved
in each month in each year from 1857.
1857/58-1857/1915.
Issued by Poor Law Board, 1857/58-
1870/71.

Poor IV.4; Poor law IV.17

643
Poor relief (England and Wales). Statement of the amount expended by Boards
of Guardians for poor relief during the
half-year . . . 1880-1913.
Title varies: Cost of relief. Statement . . .

Poor IV.4; Poor law IV.5

644
Statement showing for England and
Wales the amount of the receipts, expenditure and outstanding loans of the
principal classes of local authorities.
1910/11-1913/14.

Local government IV.1

645

Unemployed Workmen Act 1905 . . .
Return as to the proceedings of distress
committees in England and Wales and
of the Central (Unemployed) Body for
London under the Unemployed Workmen Act 1905 . . . 1-9, 1905/6-1913/14.
Unemployment IV.4

646

Vaccination. Return showing in respect
of each Poor Law Union in England
and Wales (1) the number of certificates
of conscientious objection . . . (2) . . .
certificates of successful primary vaccination . . . 1898-1900/1.
Vaccination

Local Government Board for Scotland

Set up by the Local Government (Scotland) Act 1894, replacing the Board of
Supervision. It was dissolved in 1919,
all its powers being transferred to the
*Scottish Board of Health.

647

Allotments (Scotland). Return showing
the proceedings of parish councils in
regard to allotments and common pas-
ture . . . 1901-1906/9.
*Allotments and small holdings
(Scotland)*

648

Annual report . . . 1-25, 1894/95-1918/
19.
Superseded by: Scottish Board of
Health. Annual report.
Local government (Scotland)

649

Paupers and dependants (Scotland). Return showing the number of all ordinary
poor and their dependants chargeable to
parish councils . . . 1906/7-1907/8.
Poor law (Scotland) IV.2

650

Unemployed Workmen Act 1905. Report . . . on the proceedings of distress
committees in Scotland . . . 1905/6-
1913/14.
Unemployment (Scotland)

London. Chamberlain

651

Chamber of London. Annual accounts
of the Chamberlain of the City of
London . . . 1812/13-1914/15.
Later accounts not issued as govern-
ment publications.
Not issued: 1825/26-1840/41(?).
*London (city and port) 5;
London IV.3; IV.4*

London. Imperial College of Science and Technology

652

Annual report . . . 1-32, 1907/8-1938/39.
Later reports not issued as govern-
ment publications.
PP: 1-7, 1907/8-1913/14.
NP: 8-32, 1914/15-1938/39.
Imperial College of Science

London. National Gallery and Tate Gallery

653

Directors' reports . . . 1855/64-1937.
To 1930: National Gallery, Trafalgar
Square and Millbank. Continued by
separate series of reports (both NP) for:
National Gallery, 1938/54+; and: Tate
Gallery, 1954/55+.
PP: 1855/64-1920.
NP: 1922-1937.
Not issued: 1921.
National Gallery

London. National Portrait Gallery

654

Annual report of the trustees . . . 1,
1857/58+.
PP: 1-63, 1857/58-1919/20.
NP: 64, 1920/21+.
National Portrait Gallery

London. Royal College of Art

655
Report . . . 1908/9.
Earlier, see: Board of Education. Report . . . on the Victoria and Albert Museum, the Royal College of Science and Art, etc. . . . 1901-1907.
Later reports not issued as government publications.
Royal College of Art

London Electricity Board

Established under the Electricity Act 1947.

656
Report and accounts . . . 1, 1948/49+.
Electricity

London Transport Board

Established under Transport Act 1962, assuming some of the functions of the *British Transport Commission.

657
Annual report and accounts. 1, 1963+.

Lord Chancellor's Office

The Lord Chancellor is the principal legal adviser of the Crown, and the Speaker of the House of Lords. He is in charge of a large group of offices and branches concerned with legal practice and procedure. He controls the personnel of the courts of law; appoints members of the *Law Commission and the *Council on Tribunals; and is responsible for the administration of the *Land Registry, the *Public Trustee Office, and the *Public Record Office.

658
Account of receipts and expenditure of the High Court and Court of Appeal . . . 1878/80+.
Supersedes Accounts of several divisions previously issued separately.
Court of Appeal accounts first included 1923/24.
PP: 1878/80-1922/23, 1967/68+.
NP: 1923/24-1966/67.
High Court of Justice;
Courts of law IV.3

659
Annual report of the Keeper of Public Records on the work of the Public Record Office and . . . Report of the Advisory Council on Public Records. 1959+.
Earlier, see: Public Record Office. Annual report of the Deputy Keeper . . .
PP: 9, 1967+.
NP: 1-8, 1959-1966.

660
Commissioners of Assize. Return showing the number of Commissioners of Assize appointed by the Lord Chancellor . . . the cost of such appointments, and the reasons therefore . . . 1923/24-1937/38.
Not issued: 1925/26-1927/28, 1935/36.
Assizes and quarter sessions

661
Judicial statistics, England and Wales . . . Civil judicial statistics . . . 1922+.
Continues, in part: Home Office. Judicial statistics.
Judicial statistics;
Judicial statistics, civil

662
Legal aid and advice. Report of the Law Society and comments and recommendations of the Lord Chancellor's Advisory Committee . . . 1, 1951+.
PP: 17, 1966/67+.
NP: 1-16, 1951-1965/66.

Lunacy Commission

Established by the Lunatics Act 1945. Under the Mental Deficiency Act 1913 the Commission was replaced by the *Board of Control.

663
Lunacy. Copy of the . . . report . . . 1-68, 1846-1913/14.

Continued by: Board of Control. Lunacy and Mental Treatment Acts. Annual report . . .
PP: 1-64, 1846-1909/10; 65-68, 1910/ 11-1913/14, Pt. I.
NP: 65-68, 1910/11-1913/14, Pt. II (Appendix and Index).

Lunacy

Man-made Fibres Producing Industry Training Board

Established February 1966 under Industrial Training Act 1964.

664
Report and statement of accounts . . . 1966+.

Marine Biological Association of the United Kingdom

665
North Sea fishery investigation. Southern area. Report. 1-4, 1902/3-1909.
For Report on Northern area, see: Fishery Board for Scotland.
See also: Delegates to International Hydrographic Conferences.

Fisheries III.10(c)

Marshall Aid Commemoration Commission

Constituted under the Marshall Aid Commemoration Act 1953, to administer a scheme of scholarships in Britain for United States graduate students.

666
Annual report. 1, 1953/54+.

Marshall Aid Commemoration

Medical Research Council

Incorporated by Royal Charter in April 1920, replacing the *National Health Insurance Joint Committee. Medical Research Committee.

667
Annual report . . . 1919/20+.
Combined reports issued for 1939/45, 1945/48, 1948/50.
PP: 1919/20, 1926/27+.
NP: 1920/21-1925/26.

Medical research

Merseyside and North Wales Electricity Board

Established under the Electricity Act 1947.

668
Report and accounts . . . 1, 1948/49+.

Electricity

Meteorological Office

Established in 1854, as a Department of the *Board of Trade, and has been subject to many administrative changes and changes in title. From 1867-1877, it was the Meteorological Committee of the Royal Society; 1877/78-1904/5, the Meteorological Council; 1905/6-1919/ 20, the Meteorological Committee. In 1919 the Meteorological Office was attached to the *Air Ministry, and in 1964 to the *Ministry of Defence. The Office provides the national weather service, is responsible for seismological observations, and conducts research in these fields.

669
Annual report . . . 1857+.
PP: 1857-1919/20.
NP: 1920/21+.
Not issued: 1939-1945.

Meteorology

Metropolitan Police Office

670
Metropolitan Police Fund . . . Accounts . . . 1830-1939/40.

Police

671
Report of the Commissioner of Police of the metropolis . . . 1869+.
Not issued: 1940-1942.
Police

Metropolitan Water Board

672
Report . . . 1-8, 1903/4-1910/11.
Later reports not issued as government publications.
London III.12

Midlands Electricity Board

Established under the Electricity Act 1947.

673
Report and accounts . . . 1, 1948/49+.
Electricity

Mines Department

Established by the Mining Industry Act 1920, and initially headed by a Parliamentary Secretary of the Board of Trade with the title of Secretary for Mines. Abolished in 1942, its powers being transferred to the *Ministry of Fuel and Power.

674
Coal mining industry. Annual statistical summary of output . . . 1933-1938.
Continued by: Ministry of Fuel and Power. Coal mining industry. Annual statistical statement of the costs of production . . . 1945-1946.
Coal industry IV.19(b)

675
Coal output. Return relating to the weekly output of coal . . . May 31, 1919-Sept. 24, 1921.
Coal industry IV.19(e)

676
Coal output. Statistical summary . . . 1920-June 1939.

Quarterly. Continued by: Ministry of Fuel and Power. Coal mining. Quarterly statistical statement of output . . . 1944-1946.
Coal industry IV.19(a)

677
Coal output (monthly statistics). Return relating to the output of coal . . . June 1919-Oct. 1921.
Coal industry IV.19(c)

678
Coal tables . . . Statistical tables showing the production, consumption and import and export of coal. 1-19, 1883/93-1924.
1-18, 1883/93-1912, issued by Board of Trade.
Not issued: 1913-1923.
Coal industry IV.19(a)

679
Mines and quarries: annual general reports and statistics . . . 1894-1920, Pt. 3
Pt. 1-3 continued by: Mines Department. Annual report . . . (NP)
Pt. 4, Colonial and foreign statistics, in PP only to 1912; then continued by: Imperial Mineral Resources Bureau. Mineral industry of the British Empire and foreign countries . . . (NP)
Issued by Home Office to 1919.
PP: 1894-1920, Pt. 2.
NP: 1920, Pt. 3.
Mines III.1; III.10

680
Mines and quarries: Reports of H.M. Inspectors of Mines . . . 1851-1938.
Issued by Home Office to 1914.
PP: 1851-1914.
NP: 1920-1938.
Not issued: 1915-1919.
Mines III.2; III.1

Ministry of Agriculture and Fisheries

Established 1919, replacing the *Board of Agriculture and Fisheries. In 1955 it was amalgamated with the *Ministry of Food to form the *Ministry of Agriculture, Fisheries and Food.

681
Annual report of proceedings under the

Diseases of Animals Acts, the Markets and Fairs (Weighing of Cattle) Acts, etc. . . . 1894-1938/47.

Preceded by: Veterinary Department. Annual report . . .

Note also its similar: Return of proceedings under the Diseases of Animals Act 1950 . . . (NP)

PP: 1894-1914.

NP: 1915-1938/47.

Cattle and livestock

682

Annual report of proceedings under the Small Holdings and Allotments Acts 1909 . . . Pt. 1, Small holdings . . . 1908-1914.

Continued as its: Land settlement in England and Wales . . . 1919/24, and then: Ministry of Agriculture and Fisheries. Land Division. Report . . . 1926-1937. (Both NP)

Land, etc. III.9

683

Annual report of proceedings under the Small Holdings and Allotments Acts 1909 . . . Pt. II, Allotments and miscellaneous . . . 1908-1920.

Continued as its: Report of proceedings under the Allotments Acts . . . 1924-1926, then: Ministry of Agriculture and Fisheries. Land Division. Report . . . 1926-1937. (Both NP)

PP: 1908-1914.

NP: 1920.

Not issued: 1915-1919.

Land, etc. III.9

684

Annual report of proceedings under the Tithe, etc. Acts, the Copyhold Act 1894, the Inclosure Acts, the Metropolitan Commons Acts, the Drainage and Improvement of Lands Acts, the Universities and College Estate Acts, the Glebe Lands Act 1888, etc. . . . 1889-1925.

1915/18 covered by single report.

PP: 1889-1919.

NP: 1920-1925.

Land, etc. III.7; III.11

685

Annual report of the Chief Veterinary Officer . . . 1912-1919.

Earlier and later in its: Annual re-

port of proceedings under the Diseases of Animals Acts . . .

PP: 1912-1914.

NP: 1915-1919.

Animals III.2

686

British Sugar (Subsidy) Acts 1925 to 1935. Statements, in the form of balance sheets . . . of companies which manufactured in Great Britain, sugar and molasses from home-grown beet . . . 1924/25-1935/36.

1925/26-1935/36 each in 2 parts: I. Factories; II. Refineries.

Sugar

687

Land Fertility (Research) Fund. Account . . . 1937/38-1952/53.

Land, etc. IV.4; Agriculture

688

Report of proceedings under the Small Holding Colonies Acts 1916, 1918, and Sailors and Soldiers (Gifts for Land Settlement) Act 1916. 1917-1923/26.

PP: 1917-1918/20.

NP: 1920/21-1923/26.

Allotments and small holdings III.3

689

Report on development schemes . . . 1934-1937.

Issued jointly by Ministry of Agriculture and Fisheries, Scottish Office, and Home Office.

Agriculture III.4

690

Report on sea fisheries. 1886-1937.

Issued by Board of Trade, 1886-1902.

PP: 1886-1915/18.

NP: 1919-1937.

Fisheries III.14; III.18

691

Representative authorities. Minutes of proceedings at the . . . annual meeting of representatives of sea fisheries authorities under the Sea Fisheries Regulation Act 1888. 14-28, 1904-1921.

Title varies: 14-25, . . . Report of proceedings . . .

PP: 14-27, 1904-1920.

NP: 28, 1921.
Not issued: 1-13.

Fisheries III.12

692
Salmon and freshwater fisheries ...
Report. 1862-1937.
    1862-1902 issued by Board of Trade.
PP: 1862-1915/18.
NP: 1919-1937.

Fisheries III.13; III.14

**Ministry of Agriculture and Fisheries.
Flax Production Branch**

693
Annual report. 1918-1919/20.

Flax and tow

**Ministry of Agriculture, Fisheries
and Food**

Formed in 1955 by the amalgamation
of the *Ministry of Agriculture and
Fisheries with the *Ministry of Food.

694
Agricultural statistics. United Kingdom.
1867+.
    Title varies: Agricultural returns ...
1867-1901. Issued by Board of Trade to
1882; by Agricultural Department of the
Privy Council, 1884-1888; then by Board
of Agriculture.
    1921-1938 statistics are for England
and Wales, though some also have summary for the United Kingdom. From
1939/44, two series of statistics are
issued, one for United Kingdom, one
for England and Wales, both NP.
    PP: 1867-1920.
    NP: 1921+.

Agriculture IV.13; IV.21

695
Agriculture Act 1947. Agricultural Land
Commission. Accounts...of the manage-
ment and the farming of land by the
Agricultural Land Commission and the
Welsh Agricultural Land Sub-Commis-
sion ... 1948/49-1963.

Agriculture

696
Covent Garden Market Acts 1961 and
1966. Account ... 1961/62+.

697
Herring Industry Acts 1935 to 1957.
Sea Fish Industry Act 1962. Accounts
... of the Herring Marketing Fund and
... the Herring Industry Board ...
1935/36+.
    1935/36-1944/45, Herring Fund Ad-
vances account ...

Fisheries IV

698
Miscellaneous Financial Provisions Act
1955. Potato Marketing Board. Account ... 1955/56-1959/60.

Potato Marketing Board

699
Report on agricultural marketing schemes
... 1933+.
    Issued jointly by Ministry of Agricul-
ture, Fisheries and Food; Department of
Agriculture and Fisheries for Scotland;
and Home Office; pursuant to Agricultural Marketing Act 1931.
    PP: 1934/35+.
    NP: 1933.

Agriculture III

700
Sugar Act 1956. Account ... 1956/57+.

Sugar

701
Sugar Act 1956. Home Grown Sugar
Beet (Research and Education) Fund.
Account ... 1957/58+.
    Supersedes its: Sugar Industry (Re-
search and Education) Fund. Account...

Sugar

702
Sugar Act 1956. Sugar Board. Accounts
... 1956/57+.

Sugar

703
Sugar Industry (Research and Education)
Fund. Account ... 1939/40-1956/57.
    Superseded by its: Home Grown Sugar
Beet (Research and Education) Fund.
Account ...

Sugar

Ministry of Defence

Established in January 1947, by the Ministry of Defence Act 1946, to apportion available resources between the three fighting Services and to settle questions of general administration or common policy. In 1964, by the Defence (Transfer of Functions) Act, the *Admiralty, the *Air Ministry, and the *War Office all became Departments of the Ministry of Defence.

704
Defence estimates. 1964/65+.
   Supersedes estimates previously issued separately by the Ministry and the three fighting Services. Supplementary estimates, when needed, are issued by the specific Department.

705
Defence statistics . . . 1957/58-1959/60.
   Later included as Appendix to its: Statement on the Defence estimates . . .
                                                    Defence

706
Disposal of surplus United States Mutual Defence Programme equipment. Account . . . 1960/61+.

707
Statement on the Defence estimates . . . 1935+.
   Title varies.
   From 1960, includes Appendix on Defence statistics for the coming year. From 1963, incorporates information previously found in Memoranda separately issued by each of the fighting Services to accompany their Defence estimates.
   Not issued: 1940-1945, 1947-1948.
                                                    Defence

708
Supplementary estimate. Defence (Central). 1950/51+.
   Title varies: to 1963/64, Supplementary estimate. Ministry of Defence.
                                                    Defence

Ministry of Defence. Air Force Department

709
Supplementary estimate. Defence (Air). Estimate of the further sum required to be voted for Air Services . . . 1963/64+.
   Earlier, under Air Ministry.

Ministry of Defence. Army Department

710
Royal Hospital, Chelsea. Army prize money and legacy funds, etc. . . . Account . . . 1876/77+.
   Title varies:
                                        Chelsea Hospital

711
Supplementary estimate. Defence (Army). 1963/64+.
   Earlier, under War Office.

712
Supplementary estimate. Defence (Royal Ordnance Factories). Estimate of the further sum required to be voted . . . 1964/65+.
   Earlier, under War Office.

713
Territorial and Auxiliary Forces Associations. Statement showing the financial position . . . 1908/10+.
   Title varies: Territorial Force (County Associations) . . . ; Territorial Army finance . . .
   Not issued: 1915-1920, 1939-1950.
                                    Army V.45; Armed forces IV

Ministry of Defence. Navy Department

714
Greenwich Hospital and Travers Foundation. Accounts . . . 1870+.
   Travers Foundation Accounts included from 1892/93.
                                        Greenwich Hospital

715
Greenwich Hospital and Travers Foundation. Statement of the estimated in-

come and expenditure . . . 1870/71+.

Travers Foundation included from 1893/94; a separate Statement for Travers Foundation was issued 1892/93.

Greenwich Hospital

716
Supplementary estimate. Defence (Navy). Estimate of the further sum required to be voted . . . 1966/67+.

Earlier, under Admiralty.

Ministry of Education

Established by the Education Act 1944, replacing the *Board of Education. In 1964 the Ministry of Education and the Office of the Minister for Science were merged to form the *Department of Education and Science.

717
Education in . . . Report of the Ministry of Education for England and Wales . . . 1947-1963.

Continues: Board of Education. Report . . . 1899/1900-1938.

Superseded by: Department of Education and Science. Education and science in . . . Being a report of the Department . . . 1964+.

Education and schools

718
Memorandum on the Ministry of Education estimates . . . 1922/23-1958/59.

Education and schools IV.32

Ministry of Food

Set up in December 1916 under the New Ministries and Secretaries Act; dissolved in April 1921, its residual functions being transferred mainly to the *Board of Trade. Reestablished in September 1939 under the Ministers of the Crown (Emergency Appointments) Act. In 1955 it was amalgamated with the *Ministry of Agriculture and Fisheries to form the *Ministry of Agriculture, Fisheries and Food.

719
Financial report . . . 1917/18-1918/19.

Food IV.11

Ministry of Fuel and Power

Established in June 1942 under the Ministers of the Crown (Emergency Appointments) Act 1939. It drew most of its functions from the *Board of Trade and also absorbed the *Mines Department. In January 1957 it was renamed the *Ministry of Power.

720
Coal mining. Quarterly statistical statement of output . . . 1944-1946.

Continues: Mines Department. Coal output. Statistical summary . . . 1920-1939.

Coal industry IV.19(a)

721
Coal mining industry. Annual statistical statement of the costs of production . . . 1945-1946.

Continues: Mines Department. Coal mining industry. Annual statistical summary of output . . . 1933-1938.

Coal industry IV.19(b)

722
Statistical digest . . . 1944-1946/47.

Fuel and power

Ministry of Health

Established by the Ministry of Health Act 1919, taking over all powers of the *Local Government Board and some health functions from other departments. Merged November 1968 with the *Ministry of Social Security to form the Department of Health and Social Security.

723
Annual report . . . 1919/20-1967.

Supersedes: Local Government Board. Annual report . . .

1945/46-1948/49 includes its: On the state of the public health. Annual report of the Chief Medical Officer . . . 1945-1948. (Issued separately before and after)

Not issued: 1939/40.
Summary reports issued: 1940/41-
1945/46.
Health, public III.1; Health III

724
Bedwellty Union. Board of Guardians.
Report . . . 1927-1927/28.
Poor law III.2

725
Chester-le-Street Union. Board of Guard-
ians. Report . . . 1926-1927.
Poor law III.4

726
Health Visiting and Social Work (Training) Act 1962. Council for the Training
of Health Visitors. Council for Training
in Social Work. Accounts . . . 1962/64+.
The Councils were established in
October 1962.

727
Hospital Endowments Fund. Account
. . . 1948/49+.
Hospitals

728
National Health Service Acts 1946 to
1961. Accounts . . . Summarised accounts of Regional Hospital Boards . . .
for England and Wales . . . 1948/49+.
Health IV

729
On the state of the public health. An-
nual report of the Chief Medical Officer
. . . 1919/20+.
Continues: Local Government Board.
Annual report of the Chief Medical
Officer . . .
1945-1948 included in: Ministry of
Health. Annual report . . . 1946-1948/
49.
PP: 1919/20-1920/21, 1949-1961.
NP: 1921/22-1939/45, 1962+.
Health, public III.6; Health III

730
Persons in receipt of poor relief (England and Wales). Return . . . 1879/80-
1948.
Issued by Local Government Board,
1879/80-1919, as Poor relief (Annual
returns) . . .
Not issued: 1940-1945.
Poor, etc. IV.4; Poor law IV.15

731
Unemployed persons in receipt of dom-
iciliary poor law relief in England and
Wales during the week . . . 1927-1929.
Ministry also issued quarterly: Poor
law relief. Statement showing the number of persons in receipt . . . 1916-June
1937 (NP)
Poor law IV.21

732
West Ham Union. Board of Guardians.
Report . . . 1-3 , 1926-1927/28.
Poor law III.17

Ministry of Health.
Housing Department

733
Housing. Schemes submitted . . . by local authorities and public utilities societies . . . 1-12, 1919-1920.
Housing IV.25

Ministry of Housing and
Local Government

Established in January 1951 as the
Ministry of Local Government and Planning, assuming the functions of the
Ministry of Town and Country Planning
and some functions from the *Ministry
of Health. The present title was adopted
in November 1951.

734
Alkali, etc. Works Regulation Act 1906
and Alkali, etc. Works Order 1966 . . .
Annual report by the Chief Inspectors
. . . 1, 1864+.
Agency varies: 1864-1919, Local Gov-
ernment Board; 1920-1949, Ministry of
Health; 1950, Ministry of Local Govern-
ment and Planning.
PP: 1-51, 1864-1914.
NP: 52, 1915+.
A single report was issued covering
1939/45.
Alkali works

735
House Purchase and Housing Act 1959. Accounts . . . 1959/60+.

736
Housing Act 1961. Housing (Scotland) Act 1962. Accounts prepared pursuant to Section 7(7) of the Housing Act 1961, and Section 11(7) of the Housing (Scotland) Act 1962, of the sums received by the Minister of Housing and Local Government, the Secretary of State for Scotland and the Secretary of State for Wales from the Consolidated Fund and from housing associations . . . 1962/63+.
1962/63 Account issued by Ministry of Housing and Local Government only, under Housing Act 1961. Account for Scotland added 1963/64, for Wales 1965/66.

737
Housing Act 1964. Accounts prepared pursuant to section 10(4) of the Housing Act 1964 of the sums received by the Minister of Housing and Local Government, the Secretary of State for Scotland and the Secretary of State for Wales from the Consolidated Fund and from the Housing Corporation . . . 1964/65+.
Wales included from 1965/66; Scotland added 1966/67.

738
Housing return for England and Wales. Jan. 1946-Sept. 1966.
Issued by Ministry of Health to Sept. 1950; by Ministry of Local Government and Planning, Dec. 1950-June 1951.
Monthly Jan. 1946-June 1948, then quarterly Sept. 1948-Sept. 1966.
Housing IV.17

739
Housing summary. July 1948-May 1967.
Issued by Ministry of Health, July 1948-Nov. 1950; by Ministry of Local Government and Planning, Jan.-Aug. 1951.
Issued jointly with Scottish Development Department and Welsh Office.
Monthly except March, June, Sept., Dec., in which months the quarterly Housing return was issued.
Housing IV.27

740
Local Government Act 1933. Local government financial statistics. England and Wales. 1860/61+.
Title varies: to 1933/34, Local taxation returns (England and Wales) . . .
Agency varies: 1860/61 - 1869/70, Home Office; 1870/71-1914/15, Local Government Board; 1919/20-1948/49, Ministry of Health; 1949/50, Ministry of Local Government and Planning.
PP: 1860/61-1912/13, 1913/14, Pt. 7 (Summary); 1914/15 (Summary only); 1919/20, Pt. 1.
NP: 1913/14, Pt. 1-6; 1919/20, Pt. 2-3; 1920/21+.
Not issued: 1915/16-1918/19; 1937/38-1940/41.
Summary only issued; 1941/42.
Local taxation IV.2; IV.1, 9

741
Local Government Finance (England and Wales). The Rate Support Grant Order. Report by the Minister . . . 1967/69+.

742
Mineral Workings Act 1951. Account of the Ironstone Restoration Fund . . . 1951/53+.
Ironstone Restoration Fund

743
New Towns Act . . . Reports of the Development Corporations . . . 1947/48+.
Number of Corporations included varies. From 1962/63, Crawley and Hemel Hempstead are transferred to: Commission for the New Towns. Report.
1947/48-1949/50 issued by Ministry of Town and Country Planning.
Town and country planning; New towns

744
New Towns Acts 1946 to 1966. Accounts . . . 1947/48+.
1947/48-1948/49 by Ministry of Town and Country Planning; 1949/50 by Ministry of Local Government and Planning, and Department of Health for Scotland; 1950/51-1959/60 by Ministry of Housing and Local Government, and Department of Health for Scotland.
Town and country planning; New towns

744a
Rate rebates in England and Wales . . .
1967/68+.

745
Rates and rateable values in England
and Wales. Local rates . . . Statement . . .
1913/14+.
   Agency varies: 1913/14-1949/50, Ministry of Health; 1950/51, Ministry of
Local Government and Planning.
   PP: 1913/14-1920/22.
   NP: 1921/23+.
   Not issued: 1914/15-1918/20, 1939/
40-1943/44.
                                Rates IV.5

746
Report . . . 1, 1950/54+.
                                Housing

747
Town and Country Planning Acts 1954,
1959 and 1962. Town and Country
Planning (Scotland) Acts 1954 and 1959.
Accounts . . . 1954/55+.
   Issued jointly by Ministry of Housing
and Local Government, and Scottish
Development Department.
   Town and country planning (Scotland)

748
Town and Country Planning (The Planning Payments [War Damage] Schemes
1949). Account . . . of payments under
Section 56 of the Town and Country
Planning (Scotland) Act 1947 . . . 1951/
52-1967/68.
   Irregular.
   Title varies: . . . payments by the Central Land Board under Section 59 of the
Town and Country Planning Act 1947,
and Section 56 of the Town and Country
Planning (Scotland) Act 1947.
   Discontinued under National Loans
Act 1968, future payments to be made
out of the Votes of the Ministry of
Housing and Local Government, the
Scottish Development Department, and
the Welsh Office.
   Town and country planning

Ministry of Labour

Created in January 1917 under the New

Ministries and Secretaries Act 1916,
assuming a wide variety of functions
related to employment, trade unions,
etc., from the *Board of Trade. From
1938 to 1959 its title was changed to
Ministry of Labour and National Service.
In 1968 it became the *Department of
Employment and Productivity.

749
Annual report. 1923/24-1960.
   1939/46 covered by a single report.
                                Labour III.1

750
Directory of employers' associations,
trade-unions, joint organisations, etc. 1,
1900+.
   Irregular.
   Title varies: 1900, Directory of industrial associations . . . ; 1914, Industrial directory of the United Kingdom . . .
   PP: 1900-1914, 1919.
   NP: 1917, 1925+.
                                Labour IV.3

751
Report of proceedings under the Conciliation Act 1896 . . . 1-12, 1896/97-
1914/18.
   1-11 issued by Board of Trade as:
Conciliation (Trade Disputes) Act 1896.
Report . . .
   Continued by: Ministry of Labour.
Report on conciliation and arbitration
. . . 1919-1920.
                     Arbitration; Trade boards III.1

752
Report on conciliation and arbitration
including particulars of proceedings under the Conciliation Act 1896. 1919-
1920.
   Continues its: Report of proceedings
under the Conciliation Act . . .
                                Trade boards III.2

753
Standard time rates of wages and hours
of labour in Great Britain and Northern
Ireland. 1900-1929.
   Irregular.
   Later, see its: Time rates of wages
and hours of labour . . . 1946+. (NP)
   PP: 1900-1920.
   NP: 1929.
                                Wages and hours III.5

Ministry of Labour. Statistics Division

754
Abstract of labour statistics. 1-22, 1893/94-1922/36.

Title varies: 1-5, Annual report of the Labour Department; with abstract of labour statistics.

Not issued: 1916-1925.

Labour III.3; IV.6

Ministry of Materials

Established 1951, assuming some functions of the Ministry of Supply and the *Board of Trade. Dissolved in August 1954, its functions being transferred to the *Board of Trade.

755
U.K.—Dominion Wool Disposals, Ltd. Accounts of the Joint Organisation . . . 1945/47-1953/54.

Issued by Board of Trade, 1945/47-1949/50.

Wool

Ministry of Munitions

Established in June 1915 to handle problems of wartime munitions supply. Control of ordnance factories was transferred to the *War Office in June 1920, and the Ministry was dissolved in April 1921.

756
Return of cases heard before munitions tribunals. 1915-July 1916.

Munitions III.11

Ministry of Munitions. Health of Munition Workers' Committee

757
Memorandum . . . 1-21, 1915-1918.

Munitions III.3, 4

Ministry of National Insurance

Established in April 1945 by the Ministry of National Insurance Act 1944, which transferred to it insurance responsibilities of the *Ministry of Health and the *Ministry of Labour. In 1953 it was amalgamated with the *Ministry of Pensions to form the *Ministry of Pensions and National Insurance.

758
Employers' liability insurance. Undertaking given by the Accident Offices Association . . . and certificate of the auditors . . . showing the effect of the undertaking . . . 1924-1946.

Issued by Home Office to 1944/45.

Workmen's compensation IV.3

759
Report. 1-4, 1944/49-1952.

Insurance, National III

Ministry of Overseas Development

The Ministry was established in 1964, to centralize the administration of overseas aid programs under a single Cabinet Minister, taking most of its functions from the *Colonial Office and the Department of Technical Co-operation.

760
Colonial Development and Welfare Acts 1959 to 1965. Accounts . . . 1959/60-1967/68.

1959/60-1962/63 issued jointly by Colonial Office and Commonwealth Relations Office; 1963/64 by Commonwealth Relations Office.

Discontinued under National Loans Act 1968; to be included in future in Appropriation accounts.

761
Commonwealth Education Conference. Report . . . 1, 1959+.

1, 1959, issued by Commonwealth Relations Office; 2, 1962, by Ministry of Education; 3, 1965, by Department of Education and Science.

Colonies

762
Malta (Reconstruction) Act 1947. Account . . . 1948/49+.

Issued by Colonial Office 1948/49-1963/64; by Commonwealth Office 1964/65.

Malta

763
Overseas Aid Act 1966. Account . . . in respect of the Asian Development Bank . . . 1966/67+.

764
Overseas Resources Development Acts 1959 and 1963. Account . . . of the receipts and payments of the Minister of Overseas Development in respect of the Commonwealth Development Corporation . . . 1947/48-1967/68.

Title varies: to 1962/63, . . . Colonial Development Corporation . . .

Issued by Colonial Office 1947/48-1960/61, by Commonwealth Relations Office 1961/62-1963/64.

Includes Accounts of the Overseas Food Corporation 1947/48-1950/51, and the Queensland-British Food Corporation 1951/52-1952/53.

Discontinued under National Loans Act 1968; to be included in future in Appropriation accounts.
Overseas resources; Colonies

765
Report on the . . . Commonwealth Medical Conference . . . 2, 1968+.

No report was issued on the 1st Conference, 1965, but a brief Communiqué was issued.

Ministry of Pensions

Established in February 1917 by the Ministry of Pensions Act 1916. In 1953 it was merged with the *Ministry of National Insurance to form the *Ministry of Pensions and National Insurance.

766
Report . . . 1-28, 1917/18-1952/53.

The 23rd Report covers the years 1939/48.

Superseded by: Ministry of Pensions and National Insurance. Report . . .
Pensions (naval and military and Air Force) III.1; Pensions III

Ministry of Pensions and National Insurance

Established in 1953 by the amalgamation of the *Ministry of Pensions and the *Ministry of National Insurance. In 1966 it was replaced by the *Ministry of Social Security.

767
Report . . . 1953-1965.
Pensions III

Ministry of Power

Established in January 1957, replacing the *Ministry of Fuel and Power.

768
Capital investment in the coal, gas and electricity industries . . . 1956/57-1959/60.

Issued jointly by Ministry of Power and Scottish Home Department.
Fuel and power

769
Continental Shelf Act 1964. Report . . . 1964/65+.

770
Electricity. Report of the Minister of Power . . . 1, 1948/49+.

Earlier, see: Electricity Commission. Reports of the Electricity Commissioners . . . (NP)
Electricity

771
Gas. Report of the Minister of Power . . . 1, 1948/50+.
Gas

772
Petroleum (Production) Act 1934. Account . . . of the moneys received and expended by the Minister of Power in

respect of licences to search for and get petroleum . . . 1964/65+.

773

Reports on the circumstances attending explosions and other accidents in mines, etc. . . . 1876+.

Irregular; each Report has individual title.

1876-1919, Reports to Home Office; 1920-1939, to Mines Department by Inspector of Explosives; 1942-1954, to Ministry of Fuel and Power by Inspectors of Mines; 1955+, to Ministry of Power by Chief Inspector of Mines and Quarries.

Explosives, etc. III.3; Explosions III.4; Coal III

Ministry of Public Building and Works

The Ministry came into existence in July 1962 as the result of a change in title of the *Ministry of Works.

774

Building Control Act 1966. Report by the Minister . . . 1, 1966/68+.

Ministry of Reconstruction

Created in August 1917, under the New Ministries and Secretaries Act 1916, and abolished in June 1919, when its objects had been achieved. Reestablished from November 1943 to May 1945.

775

Report . . . 1, 1918.

No more issued.

Reconstruction

Ministry of Social Security

Created by the Ministry of Social Security Act 1966, assuming functions of the *Ministry of Pensions and National Insurance. Merged November 1968 with the *Ministry of Health to form the Department of Health and Social Security.

776

Annual report . . . 1-2, 1966-1967.

777

National Insurance Acts 1965 and 1966 . . . Accounts of the National Insurance Fund, the National Insurance (Reserve) Fund, the Industrial Injuries Fund and the National Insurance (Existing Pensioners) Fund. 1948/49+.

Accounts of several funds previously issued separately. Originally issued under 1946 Act.

Insurance, National IV

778

War pensioners. Report . . . 1953+.

Earlier, this information was included in: Ministry of Pensions. Report . . .

Issued jointly by Ministry of Social Security, Ministry of Health, and Secretary of State for Scotland.

Pensions, Armed forces

Ministry of Transport

Established by the Ministry of Transport Act 1919, assuming responsibility for railways, tramways, canals, roads, etc., from the *Board of Trade, and some powers from the *Ministry of Health. From 1941 to 1946 it became the Ministry of War Transport. In 1953 it was merged with the Ministry of Civil Aviation to form the *Ministry of Transport and Civil Aviation. A separate Ministry of Aviation was created in 1959, and the Ministry of Transport reverted to its present title.

779

British Shipping (Assistance) Act 1935. Account . . . 1935/36-1947/48.

Issued 1935/36-1938/39 by Board of Trade; 1939/40 by Ministry of Shipping; 1940/41-1944/45 by Ministry of War Transport; 1945/46-1947/48 by Ministry of Transport.

Shipping

780

Electricity (Supply) Acts 1882 to 1928. Report by the Minister of Transport respecting the applications to, and pro-

ceedings of the Minister... 1919/20-1938/39.
Continues: Board of Trade. Electric Lighting Acts... Report...
PP: 1919/20-1920/21.
NP: 1921/22-1938/39.
Electricity III.7

781
Government control of railways. Estimates of the pooled revenue receipts and expenses of the controlled undertakings... !939/40-1947.
Issued pursuant to Railway Agreement (Powers) Act 1940.
Controlled undertakings were transferred to British Transport Commission in January 1948.
Railways IV.10

782
Light Railways Acts 1896, 1912, 1921. Report of the proceedings of the Ministry of Transport... 1897-1938.
PP: 1897-1920.
NP: 1921-1938.
Railways III.10; III.11

783
Railway accidents. Report... on the safety record of the railways in Great Britain... 1870+.
Title varies: to 1965,... Report upon the accidents that occurred...
PP: 1870-1938.
NP: 1944+.
Not issued: 1939-1943.
Railways III.5(d); III.1, IV.1

784
Railway accidents. Reports by the inspecting officers of railways... of inquiries into accidents... 1854-1938.
1877-1902, 1908-July/Sept. 1915, in its: Railway accidents. Returns...; 1903-1907 as Pt. II of its: Railway accidents. Returns..., but with separate Paper number.
PP: 1854-July/Sept. 1915.
NP: 1920-1938.
Not issued; 1916-1919.
Railways III.5(c); IV.1

785
Railway accidents. Returns of accidents and casualties reported... by the several railway companies in the United

Kingdom... together with reports of the inspecting officers... upon certain accidents which were inquired into... 1846-1931.
Title varies: Jan./March 1908-July/Sept. 1915, Summary of accidents and casualties...; 1930-1931, Provisional returns...
Issued quarterly to 1920, annually 1921-1931.
PP: 1846-July/Sept. 1915.
NP: Oct./Dec. 1915-1931.
Railways II.1; III.5(c); IV.1

786
Railway returns. Preliminary statement as to the capital, traffic, receipts, and working expenditure... of the railway companies. 1902-1938.
PP: 1902-1914.
NP: 1924-1938.
Not issued: 1915-1923.
Railways IV.5

787
Railway returns. Return of the capital, traffic, receipts, and working expenditure, etc. of the railway companies of Great Britain... 1860-1938.
PP: 1860-1920.
NP:1921-1938.
Not issued: 1914-1918.
Railways IV.10; IV.4

788
Railways (staff). Return... Staff employed by the railway companies of Great Britain... 1911-1947.
Title varies: Railway companies (staff and wages). Return...
1938/44 covered by a single Return.
PP: 1911-1921.
NP: 1922-1947.
Not issued: 1914-1920.
Railways IV.25

789
Report on the administration of the Road Improvement Fund. 1-10, 1910/11-1920/21.
1-9, 1910/11-1919/20, by Road Board as: Report of the proceedings...
Continued by: Ministry of Transport and Civil Aviation. Road Fund. Report...
Roads III.3

790

Road accidents . . . 1908+.
Title varies: Street accidents caused by vehicles and horses . . .
Issued by Home Office 1908-1936.
PP: 1908-1938.
NP: 1953+.
Not issued: 1939-1952.
Accidents

791

Road Fund. Estimated commitments and payments . . . 1933/34-1935/36.
Roads IV.2

792

Roads in England. Report by the Minister of Transport . . . 1965/66+.
Preceded by its: Roads in England and Wales.

793

Roads in England and Wales. Report by the Minister of Transport . . . 1956/57-1964/65.
PP: 1957/58-1964/65.
NP: 1956/57.
Preceded by: Ministry of Transport and Civil Aviation. Road Fund. Report . . .
Continued, in part, by: Ministry of Transport. Roads in England . . .
Roads

794

Severn Bridge Tolls Act 1965. Account . . . 1966/67+.

795

Tramway orders . . . Report of . . . proceedings under the Tramways Act 1870 . . . 1900-1920.
Continues, in part: Board of Trade. Tramway and gas and water orders . . . 1872-1899.
Not issued: 1916-1918.
Tramways and trolley vehicles III.4

796

Tramways and light railways (street and road). Return . . . 1870/76-1937/38.
PP: 1879/80-1913.
NP: 1918-1937/38.
Not issued: 1914-1917.
Tramways and trolley vehicles IV.3;
IV.1

Ministry of Transport and Civil Aviation

Formed in 1953 by the merging of the *Ministry of Transport and the Ministry of Civil Aviation. A separate Ministry of Aviation was created in 1959, and responsibility for other forms of transportation again reverted to the *Ministry of Transport.

797

Road Fund. Abstract accounts . . . 1910/11-1955/56.
Title varies: to 1919/20, Road Improvement Fund.
Roads IV.3

798

Road Fund. Report on the administration of the Road Fund . . . 1920/21-1955/56.
Continues: Ministry of Transport. Report on the administration of the Road Improvement Fund.
PP: 1920/21.
NP: 1921/22-1955/56.
Not issued: 1939/40-1952/53.
Roads III.4

799

Transport Fund. Account . . . 1953-1956/57.
Transport

Ministry of Works

The title and responsibilities of this agency have changed several times. Established in 1852 as the Board of Works and Public Buildings, in 1940 it became the Ministry of Works and Buildings. In 1942, assuming town and country planning functions from the *Ministry of Health, it became the Ministry of Works and Planning. However, in the following year these functions were transferred to the new Ministry of Town and Country Planning, and the title Ministry of Works was adopted. In 1962, under the Minister of Works (Change of Style and Title) Order, it became the *Ministry of Public Building and Works.

800
Annual report . . . 1949-1950.
    Preceded by its: Summary report . . .
1945/46-1948.
Works, Ministry of

801
Building Materials and Housing Fund.
Account . . . 1945/46-1953/54.
Building

802
Housing (Temporary Accommodation)
Act 1944. Account . . . 1944/45-1955/
56.
Housing IV.1

803
Summary report . . . 1945/46-1948.
    Continued by its: Annual report . . .
Works, Ministry of

Monopolies Commission

Established in July 1948 as the Monopolies and Restrictive Practices Commission. Title changed to its present form
in 1956.

804
Report . . . 1950+.
    Reports irregular, each on a specific
subject.
Monopolies

**National Advisory Councils
for Juvenile Employment**

805
Juvenile labour. Report . . . 1-6, 1928-
1937.
    PP: 2-3, 1929-1930.
    NP: 1, 1928; 4-6, 1932-1937.
Labour III.18

National Assistance Board

Set up in 1944 as the Assistance Board,
the title being changed in 1948. Dissolved in November 1966, when the
National Assistance Scheme was re-

placed by the Supplementary Benefits
Scheme, administered by the Supplementary Benefits Commission.

806
Report . . . 1944-1965.
    A report on the Board's activities for
1966 is included in: Ministry of Social
Security. Annual report . . . 1966.
Assistance; Assistance, national

National Board for Prices and Incomes

Set up by Royal Warrant in April 1965,
to consider matters relating to the prices
charged for goods, claims, and settlements regarding pay, conditions of service, employment, etc.

807
General report . . . 1, 1965/66+.
    Also included in its numbered Report
series.

808
Report. 1, 1965+.

National Coal Board

Set up in July 1946, under the Coal
Industry Nationalisation Act 1946, to
administer the industry.

809
Report and statement of accounts . . .
1, 1946+.
Coal industry III.15

National Debt Office

Commissioners for the Reduction of the
National Debt were first appointed under the Debt Reduction Act 1786, which
established a permanent Sinking Fund
to be applied to the reduction of the
National Debt. The Office later became
responsible for the administration of
various funds.

810
County Courts. Accounts. Account of the transactions of the Accountant-General of the Supreme Court under the County Court Funds Rules . . . 1935-1964.
Title varies: County Court Fund. Account . . .
Superseded by: Exchequer and Audit Department. Funds in court in England and Wales . . .
County courts; Courts of law

811
Government annuities. Account of all moneys received on account of contracts for the grant of deferred life annuities . . . 1865-1939.
Title varies: Government insurances and annuities . . .
Government insurances and annuities; Government annuities

812
Irish Land Purchase Fund. Accounts of receipts and payments by the National Debt Commissioners . . . 1903/5+.
Land, etc. (Ireland) IV.18; III

813
Local Loans Fund. Accounts . . . 1887/88-1967/68.
Fund wound up under National Loans Act 1968; future payments to be made through the National Loans Fund.
Loans

814
Military savings banks. Account . . . 1845/47-1932/33.
PP: 1845/47-1920/21.
NP: 1921/22-1932/33.
Savings banks

815
National Debt. Papers relative to the position . . . of certain funds left in trust for the reduction of the National Debt. 1936+.
National Debt II.11

816
National Debt annuities. An account . . . 1830-1940/41.
National Debt 2; III.4; II.1

817
National Debt (Savings Banks and Friendly Societies). Account of the gross amount of all sums received and paid by the National Debt Commissioners . . . 1817/52-1920.
Savings banks

818
National Health Insurance Funds. Account showing the nature and amount of the securities held by the National Debt Commissioners . . . 1912-1948.
Continued by its: National Insurance Fund and National Insurance (Reserve) Fund. Account . . .
Insurance, National Health IV.11

819
National Insurance (Existing Pensioners) Fund. Account showing the nature and nominal amount of the securities held by the National Debt Commissioners . . . 1949-1951.
Insurance, National IV

820
National Insurance Fund and National Insurance (Reserve) Fund. Account showing the nature and nominal amount of the securities held by the National Debt Commissioners . . . 1949-1951.
Continues its: National Health Insurance Funds. Account . . .
Insurance, National IV

821
Sinking Funds. Account of the Commissioners . . . 1875/76-1954/55.
National Debt III.10; II.9; Finance IV

822
Supreme Court of Judicature. Account of the receipts and expenditure of the Accountant-General of the Supreme Court, in respect of the Funds of Suitors of the Court . . . 1885/86-1964/65.
Title varies: Suitors Fund. Account . . .
Superseded by: Exchequer and Audit Department. Funds in court in England and Wales . . .
Courts of law V.19; IV.8

823
Tithe Act 1936. Redemption Annuities Account. Accounts . . . 1936/37+.
Tithe

824
Unemployment Fund investment account. 1913-1947/48.
Insurance,
National Unemployment IV.1

National Film Finance Corporation

Established April 1949, by Cinematograph Film Production (Special Loans) Act 1949, to finance the production of British films.

825
Annual report and statement of accounts . . . 1, 1949/50+.
Cinematographs .

National Health Insurance
Commission (England)

Four Commissions were set up by the National Insurance Act 1911; for England, Ireland, Scotland, and Wales. They were not under ministerial control, but uniformity was ensured by the *National Health Insurance Joint Committee of which the chairman was a Member of Parliament. The Commissions were dissolved in 1919, their functions being transferred to the *Ministry of Health, the *Scottish Board of Health, etc.

826
Reports of decisions on appeals and applications . . . 1-5, 1914/16-1919.
Insurance, National Health III.9

827
Reports of inquiries and appeals. 1913/16-1918.
Insurance, National Health III.16

National Health Insurance
Commission (Scotland)

828
Report . . . on the administration in Scotland of the National Health Insurance

Act, Pt. I (Health Insurance) . . . 1912/13-1917/19.
1912/13-1914/17 not issued separately, but included in: National Health Insurance Joint Committee. Report . . . on the administration in England . . .
Later, see: Scottish Board of Health. Annual report . . .
Insurance, National Health III.26

National Health Insurance
Joint Committee

829
National Insurance (Health) Acts 1911 to 1918. Administration of sanatorium benefit. Return . . . 1912/13-1917/18.
Insurance, National Health IV.22

830
Report . . . on the administration in England of the National Insurance Act, Pt. 1 (Health Insurance) . . . 1912/13-1914/17.
Includes Reports on the administration in Scotland and Wales.
Later, see: Ministry of Health. Annual report . . .
Insurance, National Health III.1

National Health Insurance Joint
Committee. Medical Research
Committee

831
National health insurance . . . annual report . . . 1-5, 1914/15-1918/19.
Continued by: Medical Research Council. Annual report . . .
Insurance, National Health III.20

National Insurance Audit Department

832
National Insurance Acts 1911 to 1913. Report on the work of the National Insurance Audit Department. 1-33, 1912/14-1946.
PP: 1-7, 1912/14-1920.
NP: 8-33, 1921-1946.
Not issued: 27-31, 1940-1944.
Insurance, National Health III.5

National Parks Commission

Set up in December 1949, under the National Parks and Access to the Countryside Act, to preserve and enhance natural beauty in England and Wales.

833
National Parks and Access to the Countryside Act 1949. Report of the National Parks Commission. 1, 1949/50+.
Parks

National Ports Council

Established in June 1964, under the Harbours Act 1964, to consider major development schemes for harbours and ports.

834
Annual report and accounts. 1964+.

National Radium Trust and Radium Commission

835
Annual reports ... 1-19, 1929/30-1946/48.
Not issued: 11-15, 1940/41-1944/45; Abstracts for these years included as Appendices to 16, 1945/46.
Radium

National Relief Fund

836
Report on the administration of the National Relief Fund. 1-10, 1914/15-1919/21.
National Relief Fund

**National Relief Fund.
Scottish Advisory Committee**

837
Report on the administration of the

National Relief Fund ... 1-2, 1914/15-1915.
National Relief Fund

**National Research
Development Corporation**

Established under the Development of Inventions Act 1948 to support the development of British inventions.

838
Annual report and statement of accounts ... 1, 1949/50+.
*National Research Development
Corporation*

National Savings Committee

839
Annual report ... 1-23, 1916/17-1939.
1-3 as National War Savings Committee.
PP: 1-5, 1916/17-1920.
NP: 6-23, 1922-1939.
War, 1914-1918 III.2; National savings

Natural Environment Research Council

Council established by Royal Charter, June 1965, bringing together official bodies of life and earth scientists, including *Nature Conservancy, Geological Survey & Museum, Soil Surveys, Hydrology Research Unit, etc.

840
Report ... 1965/66+.

Nature Conservancy

Established pursuant to National Parks and Access to the Countryside Act 1949.

841
Report ... 1-15, 1949/52-1963/64.
For later information on work of Nature Conservancy, see: Natural En-

vironment Research Council. Report . . .
Nature Conservancy

North Eastern Electricity Board

Established under the Electricity Act 1947.

842
Report and accounts . . . 1, 1948/49+.
Electricity

North Eastern Gas Board

Established under the Gas Act 1948.

843
Annual report and accounts . . . 1, 1949/50+.
Gas

North of Scotland Hydro-Electric Board

Constituted under the Hydro-Electric Development (Scotland) Act 1943.

844
Report and accounts . . . 1949+.
Includes: Electricity Consultative Council for the North of Scotland District. Report . . .
Electricity (Scotland)

North Thames Gas Board

Established under the Gas Act 1948.

845
Annual report and accounts . . . 1, 1949/50+.
Gas

North Western Electricity Board

Established under the Electricity Act 1947.

846
Report and accounts . . . 1, 1948/49+.
Electricity

North Western Gas Board

Established under the Gas Act 1948.

847
Annual report and accounts . . . 1, 1949/50+.
Gas

Northern Gas Board

Established under the Gas Act 1948.

848
Annual report and accounts . . . 1, 1949/50+.
Gas

Office of the Commissioner for the Special Areas (England & Wales)

849
Report . . . 1-5, 1934/35-1938/39.
Unemployment III.3

Office of the Commissioner for the Special Areas (Scotland)

850
Report . . . 1-5, 1934/35-1938/39.
Unemployment (Scotland)

Ordnance Survey

Set up in 1791 under the Board of Ordnance, it is now administered by the *Ministry of Housing and Local Government. The Survey is in charge of the survey and mapping of Great Britain and also undertakes work for other departments, particularly the *Ministry of Defence and the *Land Registry.

851
Annual report . . . 1855/56+.
  PP: 1855/56-1920/21.
  NP: 1921/22+.
  Not issued: 1939/40-1953/54.
                    Surveys; Ordnance survey

Oversea Migration Board

Board appointed 1953 as successor to
prewar *Oversea Settlement Office.

852
Report . . . 1-7, 1954-1961.
                              Migration

853
Statistics. 1961-1964.
  Earlier, included in its: Report.

Oversea Settlement Office

Established in 1919, replacing the *Emigrants' Information Office.

854
Report . . . 1919-1938.
  Supersedes: Emigrants' Information
Office. Report . . . 1887/88-1914.
                    Overseas settlement

Overseas Food Corporation

Established under the Overseas Resources Development Act 1948, in order
to investigate and carry out projects for
food production and processing in overseas territories and to market the products. The Overseas Resources Development Act 1954 transferred the undertaking to the Tanganyika Agricultural
Corporation.

855
Annual report and statement of accounts . . . 1948/49-1954/55.
  1948/49, 1949/50, include 1st and
2nd Reports of the Queensland-British

Food Corporation, later Reports of
which were issued separately.
                Overseas resources; Colonies

Parliament. Ecclesiastical Committee

856
Report . . . 1, 1920+.
  Irregular.
                        Church of England

Parliament. House of Commons

857
Adjournment motions . . . Return . . .
1882/87-1930/31.
                    House of Commons IV.1

858
Business of the House (days occupied
by government and private members).
Return . . . 1888-1914.
  Continued, in reduced form, in its:
Return showing . . . the total number of
days on which the House sat . . .
            House of Commons IV.11; IV.3

859
Closure of debate (Standing Order XXV).
Return . . . 1887/88-1930/31.
              House of Commons IV.7; IV.4

860
Divisions. Return . . . 1842-1906.
        House of Commons III.4; IV.10; IV.5

861
General alphabetical index to the Bills,
Reports, and Papers printed by order of
the House of Commons and to the Reports and Papers presented by Command . . . 1801/26+.
  Title varies; period covered varies,
but generally decennial from 1870-
1878/79, except for 1929-1943/44 and
1944/45-1948/49. Fifty-year cumulations provide coverage from 1801 to
1948/49. The Index for 1801-1852 is in
three separate volumes: Bills; Accounts
and Papers, etc.; and Select Committees.
The 1852-1899 Index lacks Paper numbers, which are to be found in the Index

for 1852/53-1868/69 and the succeeding decennial Indexes.
Parliamentary papers

862
House of Commons Members' Fund. Accounts . . . 1939/40+.
House of Commons IV.10

863
Parliamentary papers (House of Commons and Command). Sessional index . . . 1806/7+.
Parliamentary papers

864
Petitions. Return of the number of public petitions presented and printed . . . 1874/81-1930/31.
House of Commons IV.17; IV.15

865
Private bills. Returns of the number of private bills, . . . and of acts passed in the session . . . 1847-1930/31.
Private business (House of Commons); Bills, private

866
Public bills. Return of the number of public bills . . . 1868/69+.
Not issued: 1931/32-1946/47.
Bills, public; House of Commons IV

867
Return showing . . . the total number of days on which the House sat, and the days on which business of supply was considered . . . 1914/16-1930/31.
Continues, in much less detailed form, its two publications: Sittings. Return of the number of days on which the House sat in session . . . ; and: Business of the House (days occupied by government and private members). Return . . .
House of Commons IV.3

868
Select Committees . . . Return of the number appointed in session . . . 1852/53-1930/31.
House of Commons IV.8; IV.18

869
Sittings. Return of the number of days on which the House sat in session . . . 1842-1914.
Continued, in reduced form, in its: Return showing . . . the total number of days on which the House sat . . .
Sittings of the House; House of Commons IV.21; IV.20

870
Standing Committees. Minutes of proceedings . . . 1936/37+.
Supersedes its: Standing Committees. Reports . . .
Committees are appointed each session to deal with Committee stage of Bills, the number varying according to need and most being identified only by a letter. Committees appointed for the 1967/68 session were: A-H, Report Committee, Second Reading Committee, Scottish Grand Committee, two Scottish Standing Committees, and Welsh Grand Committee.

871
Standing Committees. Reports . . . 1882-1935/36.
Some include Proceedings.
To 1907, there were two named Standing Committees: on Trade; and on Law and Courts of Justice, and Legal Procedure. From 1908, Standing Committees were identified by letter (initially A, B, C), with the addition of a Scottish Standing Committee to consider Bills relating to Scotland.
Superseded by its: Standing Committees. Minutes of proceedings . . .

872
Standing Committees. Return . . . of the total number and the names of all members . . . 1907+.
House of Commons IV.21

873
Standing orders of the House of Commons. Private business. 1801+.
House of Commons 12; IV.23; IV.23

874
Standing orders of the House of Commons. Public business. 1801+.
House of Commons 12; IV.23; IV.23

**Parliament. House of Commons.
Committee of Privileges**

875
Report . . . 1874+.
Irregular.
*House of Commons II.14; Privileges;
House of Commons II*

**Parliament. House of Commons.
Committee of Public Accounts**

876
Report . . . together with the Proceedings of the Committee, Minutes of evidence, and Appendix . . . 1861+.
Accounts, public

877
Special report . . . 1866+.
Irregular.
Accounts, public

**Parliament. House of Commons.
Estimates Committee**

878
Minutes of proceedings . . . 1947/48+.
Earlier, and 1948/49-1950, issued with its: Report . . .
To 1959/60, . . . Select Committee on Estimates.
Estimates; Estimates, Select Committee

879
Report . . . 1912/13+.
Title and contents vary: some include Proceedings, Minutes of evidence, etc. Index issued separately from 1948/49.
Not issued: 1915-1920, 1939-1944.
Estimates; Estimates, Select Committee

880
Special report . . . 1953/54+.
Estimates, Select Committee

**Parliament. House of Commons.
Estimates Committee
(Sub-Committee B)**

881
Minutes of evidence . . . 1967+.

Some not issued separately, but with Estimates Committee's Report . . .

**Parliament. House of Commons. Select
Committee on Agriculture**

882
Minutes of evidence . . . 1967+.
Also issued in its: Report . . .

883
Report, Minutes of evidence taken before the Sub-Committee . . . Appendices and Index. 1968+.

884
Special report . . . 1967+.

**Parliament. House of Commons.
Select Committee on Agriculture.
Sub-Committee on Horticulture**

885
Minutes of evidence . . . 1968+.
Also issued in the Select Committee's Report.

**Parliament. House of Commons.
Select Committee on Education
and Science**

886
Minutes of evidence . . . 1968+.
Also issued in its: Report . . .

887
Report . . . 1968+.
Includes Proceedings and Minutes of evidence.

888
Special report . . . 1968+.

**Parliament. House of Commons.
Select Committee on Expiring Laws**

889
Register of temporary laws. 1852/53-1958/59.
Laws, expiring; Laws, temporary

Parliament. House of Commons. Select Committee on House of Commons (Services)

The Committee replaces the Select Committee on Kitchen and Refreshment Rooms, and the Select Committee on Publications and Debates Reports.

890
Minutes of the proceedings . . . 1965/66+.

891
Report . . . 1965/66+.

892
Special report . . . 1965/66+.

Parliament. House of Commons. Select Committee on Kitchen and Refreshment Rooms

The Committee was normally appointed each session to consider problems relating to food services of the House. It has been replaced by the Select Committee on House of Commons (Services).

893
Special report . . . 1852/53-1964/65.
  Title varies: to 1915, Report . . .
  Not issued: 1916-1921.
      House of Commons II.7; II.9

Parliament. House of Commons. Select Committee on Local Legislation

894
Special report . . . with proceedings . . . 1909-1929/30.
      Local legislation

Parliament. House of Commons. Select Committee on Nationalised Industries

895
Minutes of proceedings . . . 1954/55+.
  Irregular as separate; often included

with its: Report . . .
      Nationalised industries

896
Report . . . 1951/52+.
  Some include Proceedings, Minutes of evidence, and Appendices.
      Nationalised industries

897
Special report . . . 1955/56+.
      Nationalised industries

Parliament. House of Commons. Select Committee on Nationalised Industries. Sub-Committee A

898
Minutes of evidence . . . 1967+.
  Also issued in the Select Committee's Report . . .

Parliament. House of Commons. Select Committee on Nationalised Industries. Sub-Committee B

899
Minutes of evidence . . . 1968+.
  Some also issued in the Select Committee's Report . . .

Parliament. House of Commons. Select Committee on Procedure

900
Report . . . 1886+.
  Irregular.
      House of Commons II.17; II.15

Parliament. House of Commons. Select Committee on Publications and Debates Reports

The Committee considered arrangements for the reporting and publishing of the Debates, publishing of the Sessional Papers, and working conditions of the staff. It was replaced by the Select Committee on House of Commons (Services).

901
Report . . . with the Proceedings of the Committee, and Minutes of evidence . . . 1906-1963/64.
House of Commons II.21

Parliament. House of Commons. Select Committee on Science and Technology

902
Report . . . Minutes of evidence, Appendices and Index. 1966/67+.
Minutes of evidence also issued separately, in parts, for each day of hearings; final part cumulates all Minutes with Report . . .

903
Special report . . . 1966/67+.

Parliament. House of Commons. Select Committee on Science and Technology. Sub-Committee on Coastal Pollution

904
Minutes of evidence . . . 1968+.

Parliament. House of Commons. Select Committee on Statutory Instruments

905
Minutes of the proceedings . . . 1943/44+.
Some also issued in its: Report . . .
Title varies: to 1947, Select Committee on Statutory Rules and Orders.
Statutory rules and orders;
Statutory instruments

906
Report . . . 1943/44+.
Some include Proceedings, Minutes of evidence, Appendices, etc. To 1950, a cumulated Report gathers all Proceedings of the session.
Statutory rules and orders;
Statutory instruments

907
Special report. 1945/46+.
To 1950, also issued in its: Report . . .
Statutory rules and orders;
Statutory instruments

Parliament. House of Commons. Select Committee on the Parliamentary Commissioner for Administration

908
Minutes of proceedings . . . 1967+.
Also issued in its: Report . . .

909
Report . . . 1968+.
Includes Proceedings and Minutes of evidence.

Parliament. House of Lords

910
Fee Fund. Account of the Fee Fund of the House of Lords. 1888/89-1930/31.
House of Lords

Parliament. Joint Committee of the House of Lords and the House of Commons . . . Appointed to Consider All Consolidation Bills . . .

911
Report . . . 1912/13+.
Some include Proceedings and Minutes of evidence.

Parliamentary Commissioner for Administration

Appointed under the Parliamentary Commissioner Act 1967, to consider complaints of injustice through maladministration referred to the Commissioner through Members of Parliament.

912
Annual report . . . 1967+.
Included in its sessionally numbered Report series.

913
Report . . . 1967+.
    Irregular.

PP: 1909/10-1914/15, 1918/19-1919/ 20.
NP: 1915/16-1917/18.

London III.14

Patent Office

The Office in its present form dates from 1883, when the Patents, Designs and Trade Marks Act abolished the Patent Commissioners appointed in 1852 and vested their powers in a Comptroller-General. The Office deals with the registration of patents and trademarks, also with copyright questions, etc.

914
Report of the Comptroller-General of Patents, Designs, and Trade Marks, with Appendices . . . 1, 1884+.
    Supersedes Report of the Commissioners of Patents.
    Not issued: 58-65, 1940/41-1947/48.
    (Typescript copies available at the Patent Office)

Patents

Petroleum Industry Training Board

Established May 1967 under Industrial Training Act 1964.

915
Report and statement of accounts . . . 1967/68+.

Port of London Authority

Established by the Port of London Act 1908 which gave to the Authority jurisdiction over the lower Thames, administration of the upper part being retained by the *Thames Conservancy Office.

916
Annual report . . . 1909/10-1919/20.
    Later Reports not issued as government publications.

Post Office

The evolution of the Post Office in its modern form began in 1657 with the establishment of the General Post Office and the appointment of a Postmaster General. The introduction of the penny post and of postage stamps in 1840 gave it an effective monopoly of postal services. Later services added were the Post Office Savings Bank in 1861, the telegraph service in 1870, and telephones and postal orders in 1881. A 1967 Report recommended the transformation of the Post Office from a Department of State to a public corporation, a change effected in October 1969.

917
American mail service. Return showing time occupied . . . 1890-1905/6.

Post Office IV.5

918
Cable and Wireless Limited. Accounts . . .   together with the report of the directors. 1946+.
    PP: 1946-1961/62.
    NP: 1962/63+.

Telegraphs, etc. IV.5

919
Independent Television Authority. Account of the sums issued to the Postmaster-General out of the Consolidated Fund . . . in respect of advances to the Independent Television Authority . . . 1954/55-1959/60.

Broadcasting

920
Post Office capital expenditure. 1959/ 60-1960/61.
    Earlier, this information was included in its: Post Office report and accounts . . .
    Superseded by its: Post Office prospects . . .

Post Office IV

921

Post Office Fund. Account . . . 1934/35-1939/40.

Post Office IV.31

922

Post Office (London) Railway Act 1913. Account showing the money issued out of the Consolidated Fund . . . 1913/14-1924/25.

Post Office IV.33

923

Post Office prospects. 1961/62+.

Supersedes its: Post Office capital expenditure.

924

Post Office report and accounts . . . 1870+.

Title varies:

1870-1918/19, Post Office. Account showing the gross amount received and expended on account of the telegraph service, from the date of the transfer of the telegraphs to the state . . .

1919/20, Post Office. Statements as regards the telegraph service . . .

1920/21-1947/48, Post Office commercial accounts . . .

1948/49-1956/57, Post Office. Commercial accounts and report . . .

1957/58-1960/61, Post Office. Report and commercial accounts . . .

Not issued: 1940/41-1946/47.

Telegraphs, etc. IV.2; Post Office IV.2

925

Report of the Postmaster General on the Post Office, 1-62, 1854-1915/16.

Post Office III.1

926

Television Act 1964. Independent Television Authority additional payments by programme contractors. Account . . . 1964/65+.

Post Office. Standing Committee on Boy Labour in the Post Office

927

Report . . . 1-5, 1911-1914.

Post Office III.2

Prison Commission

The Prison Commissioners were appointed by Royal Warrant under the Prisons Act 1877. In 1898 they were also made Directors of Convict Prisons, amalgamation of the two related bodies thus being secured. The Prison Commission was abolished in 1963, and the administration of prisons is now the responsibility of the *Home Office. Prison Department.

928

Prisons. Report of the Commissioners of Prisons . . . 1895/96-1962.

Title varies: 1895/96-1948, Report of the Commissioners of Prisons and the Directors of Convict Prisons . . .

Continues its two series, both in PP: Report of the Commissioners of Prisons . . . ; and: Report of the Directors of Convict Prisons . . .

Prisons

Prison Commissioners for Scotland

Appointed under the Prisons (Scotland) Act 1877. Under the Reorganisation of Offices (Scotland) Act 1928, the Commissioners were replaced in April 1929 by the *Prisons Department for Scotland.

929

Annual report . . . 1839-1928.

Continued by: Prisons Department for Scotland. Annual report . . .

PP: 1839-1920, 1925-1928.

NP: 1921-1924.

Prisons (Scotland)

Prisons Department for Scotland

Originally established as the Department of Prisons and Judicial Statistics; the present title was adopted in 1929 when the Department assumed the powers of the Prison Commissioners for Scotland, who ceased to exist under the Reorganisation of Offices (Scotland) Act 1928. The Department ceased to exist in September 1939, and responsibility for prisons in Scotland was transferred to the *Scottish Home Department (later the *Scottish Home and Health Department).

930
Annual report . . . 1929-1938.
  Continues: Prison Commissioners for Scotland. Annual report . . .
  Continued by: Scottish Home and Health Department. Prisons in Scotland . . .

Prisons (Scotland)

931
Report on the judicial statistics of Scotland. 1868-1924.
  Continued by two series, now issued by Scottish Home and Health Department: Criminal statistics, Scotland; and; Judicial statistics, Scotland . . . Civil . . . (Both in PP)
  PP: 1868-1914.
  NP: 1915-1924.
Statistical tables II.2;
Judicial statistics (Scotland)

Private International Law Committee

Appointed in September 1952 to consider possible alterations in private international law.

932
Report . . . 1, 1954+.
  Not issued: 2-3
Law

Public Health Laboratory Service Board

Established 1961 to administer bacteriological services provided by the *Ministry of Health under the National Health Service Act 1946, taking over these functions from the *Medical Research Council.

933
Public Health Laboratory Service Act 1960. Public Health Laboratory Service Board. Accounts . . . 1961/62+.

Public Record Office

Set up by the Public Record Office Act 1838, to provide proper accommodation for the public records and to facilitate their free use. The Office was administered by a Deputy Keeper under the supervision of the Master of the Rolls. In accordance with a 1954 Committee recommendation that the Office should be transferred to a Ministry of the Crown, a new post of Keeper of the Public Records was established in 1959, responsible to the *Lord Chancellor's Office.

934
Annual report of the Deputy Keeper of the Public Records . . . 1-120, 1839/40-1958.
  Later, see: Lord Chancellor's Office. Annual report of the Keeper of Public Records . . .
  PP: 1-76, 1839/40-1914/15.
  NP: 77-82, 1915-1920; 109-120, 1947-1958.
  Not issued: 83-108, 1921-1946 (copies available from Public Record Office).
Records

Public Trustee Office

Created by the Public Trustee Act 1906, to enable the state to act as the executor or trustee of any individual so desiring.

935
Public Trustee. Annual report . . . 1, 1908/9+.
  PP: 1-12, 1908/9-1919/20.
  NP: 13, 1920/21+.
  Not issued: 32-41, 1939/40-1948/49.
Trusts; Trustees

Public Works Loan Board

The Public Works Loan Act 1875 placed the Public Works Loan Commissioners, originally appointed in 1817, under the administration of a Board. It is responsible for the handling of advances for public works from the Consolidated Fund and other funds.

936
Annual report . . . 1, 1875/76+.
    PP: 1-46, 1875/76-1920/21.
    NP: 47, 1921/22+.
    Not issued: 65-70, 1939/40-1944/45.
                    Works, public

Queen Anne's Bounty Board

Established by Charter in 1705, with the purpose of providing funds to aid the poorer clergy. The Board was dissolved in 1948, being replaced by the Church Commissioners for England.

937
Annual report and accounts of the governors . . . 1837-1939.
    PP: 1837-1915.
    NP: 1916-1939.
              Queen Anne's Bounty

Queen's and Lord Treasurer's Remembrancer

This ancient title is that of the Treasury's representative in Scotland.

938
Ultimus Haeres (Scotland) (account and list of estates). Copy of abstract account of the receipts and payments of the Queen's and Lord Treasurer's Remembrancer in the administration of estates and treasure trove in Scotland on behalf of the Crown . . . 1886+.
    PP: 1886-1920.
    NP: 1921+.
         Ultimus Haeres (Scotland)

Queensland-British Food Corporation

Set up in April 1948, by an Act of the Queensland State Parliament, as a subsidiary of the *Overseas Food Corporation to undertake schemes for mechanized food production in Queensland. The Corporation was wound up in September 1952.

939
Report . . . 1-5, 1948/49-1951/52.
    1-2, 1948/49-1949/50, in: Overseas Food Corporation. Report . . .
    Not issued: 3, April-Sept. 1950.
                    Colonies

Race Relations Board

Established under the Race Relations Act 1965.

940
Report . . . 1, 1966/67+.

Racecourse Betting Control Board

941
Annual report and accounts. 1-11, 1929-1939.
                      Betting

Railway and Canal Commission

Set up by the Railway and Canal Traffic Act 1888 to judge complaints from local authorities, etc. Abolished by the Railway and Canal Commission (Abolition) Act 1949, its functions in England and Wales being transferred to the High Court, and in Scotland to the Court of Session.

942
Annual report . . . 1-50, 1889-1938.
    Not issued: 45, 1933.
         Railways III.1; III.14

Raw Cotton Commission

Established in January 1948, under the Cotton (Centralised Buying) Act 1947, to buy, import, and distribute all raw cotton required for the British cotton industry. The Cotton Act 1954 ended its responsibility as a monopoly supplier, and the Commission was dissolved in August 1954.

943
Annual report and statement of accounts . . . 1-7, 1948-1953/54.

Cotton; Cotton industry

Registrar of Restrictive Trading Agreements

The Restrictive Trade Practices Act 1956 requires the Registrar to maintain a register of agreements subject to registration under the Act, and to take civil proceedings to the Restrictive Practices Court.

944
Restrictive trading agreements. Report of the Registrar . . . 1956/59+.

Registry of Friendly Societies

Established in 1846, when the barrister appointed to certify rules of Friendly Societies was appointed Registrar. A central office was created in 1875.

945
Industrial assurance. Report of the Industrial Assurance Commissioner. 1-15, 1924-1938; 1952+.

Note also its: Industrial assurance. Reports of selected disputes referred to the . . . Commissioner, 1938-1949 (NP).
PP: 1-15, 1924-1938.
NP: 1952+.
Not issued: 1939-1951.

Assurance

946
Report of the Chief Registrar . . . 1875+.

Report covers the United Kingdom. Earlier, 1855-1874, separate Reports were issued in PP for England, Ireland, and Scotland.

Issued in several parts, with varying dates of issue and identified at first by letters, then by numbers, as indicated below:
General. (Pt. A, 1875-1923; Pt. 1, 1924+)
PP: 1875-1938.
NP: 1952+.
Not issued: 1939-1951.

Friendly societies

Friendly Societies. (Pt. 2, 1924+)
NP: 1924+.
Not issued: 1938-1951.

Industrial and Provident Societies. (Pt. B, 1875-1922; Pt. 3, 1924+)
PP: 1875-1914.
NP: 1915+.
Not issued: 1923, 1938-1951.

Friendly societies

Trade Unions. (Pt. C, 1875-1922; Pt. 4, 1924+)
PP: 1875-1914.
NP: 1915+.
Not issued: 1923, 1938-1951.

Friendly societies

Building Societies. (Pt. D, 1895-1922; Pt. 5, 1924+)
PP: 1895-1914.
NP: 1915+.
Not issued: 1923, 1939-1951.

Building societies

Review Body on Doctors' and Dentists' Remuneration

947
Report . . . 1, 1963+.

1-3, 6, 8, were printed in the House of Commons Parliamentary Debates (Official Report), March 25, 1963; Feb. 1, 1965; Aug. 5, 1965; and May 12, 1967.
PP: 3-5, 7, 9+.

Road Haulage Disposal Board

The Board was created under the Transport Act 1953, to report on the disposal of the property of the *British Transport Commission.

948
Report . . . 1-7, 1953-1956.
Transport

Road Transport Industry Training Board

Established September 1966 under Industrial Training Act 1964.

949
Report and statement of accounts . . .
1966/67+.

**Royal Commission of the
Patriotic Fund**

The Fund was established during the Crimean War, to provide for the families of military personnel killed on active service. The Commission was replaced in 1904 by the *Royal Patriotic Fund Corporation.

950
Report . . . 1-42, 1856-1903.
    Continued by: Royal Patriotic Fund
Corporation. Report . . .
Patriotic Fund

**Royal Commission on Awards
to Inventors**

Commission appointed to consider claims arising from 1914-1918 War.

951
Report . . . 1-7, 1919/20-1937.
    Irregular.
Inventors and inventions

**Royal Commission on Awards
to Inventors**

Commission appointed to consider claims arising from Second World War.

952
Report . . . 1-4, 1947/48-1952/55.

Irregular.
Inventors and inventions; Inventions

**Royal Commission on Defence
of the Realm Losses**

953
Report . . . 1-5, 1915/16-1919/20.
    Continued by: War Compensation
Court. Report . . . (NP)
Defence of the realm (World War I)

**Royal Commission on Historical
Manuscripts**

954
Report . . . 1, 1870+.
    Irregular.
    PP: 1-18, 1870-1917.
    NP: 19, 1926+.
Historical manuscripts

**Royal Commission on the Ancient and
Historical Monuments and Constructions
of England**

955
Interim report. 1, 1910+.
    Irregular.
*Historical monuments;
Historic buildings, etc.*

**Royal Commission on the Ancient and
Historical Monuments and Constructions
of Wales and Monmouthshire**

956
Interim report . . . 1, 1909+.
    Irregular.
*Historical monuments (Wales);
Historic buildings, etc.*

**Royal Commission on the Ancient and
Historical Monuments of Scotland**

957
Report . . . 1, 1909+.
    Irregular.

No. 6, issued in 1915, is a revised version of no. 1.

Historical monuments (Scotland);
Historic buildings, etc.

Royal Fine Art Commission

958
Report . . . 1, 1924+.
  Irregular.
Fine Art Commission; Fine art

Royal Fine Art Commission
for Scotland

The Commission was appointed in 1927, but did not issue any reports until 1960.

959
Report . . . 1, 1960+.

Royal Mint

As the agency responsible for making and issuing the nation's coinage, the Mint has existed for many centuries. As now constituted, it dates only from 1817. The Coinage Act 1870 abolished the ancient post of Master of the Mint and placed the Mint under direct control of the Chancellor of the Exchequer.

960
Annual report of the Deputy Master and Comptroller . . . 1, 1870+.
  A single Report was issued for 1939/44.
  PP: 1-44, 1870-1913.
  NP: 45, 1914+.
Coinage; Currency and coinage

Royal Patriotic Fund Corporation

The Corporation replaced the *Royal Commission of the Patriotic Fund, established in 1856 to provide for the families of military personnel killed on active service.

961
Report . . . 1-15, 1904-1918.
  Continues: Royal Commission of the Patriotic Fund. Report . . .
Patriotic Fund

Rubber and Plastics Processing
Industry Training Board

Established August 1967 under Industrial Training Act 1964.

962
Report and statement of accounts . . . 1967/68+.

Saint Andrews. University

963
Annual report on the state of the finances . . . 1889/90-1913/14.
  Title varies: Abstract of accounts . . .
Universities and colleges (Scotland)

964
Annual statistical report . . . 1898/99-1913/14.
Universities and colleges (Scotland)

Sandhurst. Royal Military College

965
Report of the Board of Visitors appointed . . . for the inspection of the Royal Military College, Sandhurst . . . 1877-1900.
Sandhurst; Army III.29

Science Research Council

Established by Royal Charter in April 1965, under the Science and Technology Act 1965, to encourage and support research and development in science and technology.

966
Report . . . 1, 1965/66+.

Scottish Board of Health

Established in July 1919, assuming all powers of the *Local Government Board for Scotland and the Scottish Insurance Commissioners, health functions of the *Scottish Education Department, and the functions in Scotland of the *Ministry of Pensions. In January 1929 it was replaced by the *Department of Health for Scotland, under the Reorganisation of Offices (Scotland) Act 1928.

967
Annual report . . . 1-10, 1919-1928.
   Continues: Local Government Board for Scotland. Annual report . . .
   Continued by: Department of Health for Scotland. Report . . .
Health, public (Scotland)

968
Housing, Town Planning, etc. (Scotland) Act 1919. Summary of returns made to the Board . . . 1920-1926/27.
   PP: 1920-1921.
   NP: 1921/22-1926/27.
Housing (Scotland) IV.12

969
Meals and milk. Return showing the percentage of school children receiving milk under the Milk in Schools Scheme . . . 1942-1945.
Education and schools (Scotland) IV.15

Scottish Development Department

Established June 1962, under the Reorganisation of Offices (Scotland) Act 1939, combining some functions of the *Department of Health for Scotland and the *Scottish Home Department, which were merged to form the *Scottish Home and Health Department.

970
Housing return for Scotland. Jan. 1946+.
   To Sept. 1961, issued by Department of Health for Scotland; Dec. 1961-March 1962, by Scottish Home and Health Department.

Monthly Jan. 1946-June 1948, then quarterly Sept. 1948+.
   PP: 1946-1966.
   NP: 1967+.
Housing (Scotland) IV.9

971
Housing (Scotland) Act 1962. Housing Act 1964. Account prepared pursuant to Sections 11(7) and 18(3) of the Housing (Scotland) Act 1962 of the sums received by the Secretary of State for Scotland from the Consolidated Fund and from the Scottish Special Housing Association . . . 1962/63+.
   1962/63-1963/64 under Housing (Scotland) Act 1962 only.

972
Industry and employment in Scotland and Scottish roads report . . . 1-17, 1949-1962/63.
   Scottish roads report omitted from 1962/63 Report.
   1949-1959/60 issued by Scottish Home Department; 1960/61 by Scottish Home and Health Department.
Scotland

973
Local Government Finance (Scotland). The Rate Support Grant (Scotland) Order . . . Report by the Secretary of State for Scotland . . . 1968/69+.

974
Rate rebates in Scotland . . . 1967/68+.

975
Rents of houses owned by local authorities in Scotland. Return . . . 1938+.
   1938-1961 issued by Department of Health for Scotland.
   Not issued: 1939-1948.
*Rent and mortgages IV.4;
Housing (Scotland)*

976
Report . . . 1, 1962+.

Scottish Education Department

Set up by the Education (Scotland) Act 1872 as a Committee of the Privy Council. Full responsibility for the Department was transferred to the Secretary of State for Scotland in 1939.

977
Annual report by the Accountant for Scotland. 1-66, 1873-1937/38.
PP: 1-48, 1873-1919/20.
NP: 49-66, 1921-1937/38.
Education and schools (Scotland) III.1; III.2

978
Code of regulations (day schools) . . . 1874-1915.
Education and schools (Scotland) IV.3; IV.5

979
Code of regulations (evening and continuation schools) . . . 1893-1915.
Education and schools (Scotland) IV.5; IV.6

980
Continuation classes. Reports, statistics, etc. . . . 1902/3-1920/21.
PP: 1902/3-1906/7.
NP: 1907/8-1920/21.
Education and schools (Scotland) III.4

981
Education in Scotland. Report . . . 1873/74+.
Numbered reports, 1-66, 1873/74-1938/39, entitled: Report of the Committee of Council on Education in Scotland . . .
Summary reports issued for 1939/40-1946.
Education and schools (Scotland) III.4; III.1

982
Education (Scotland). Minute of the Committee of Council on Education in Scotland . . . providing for the distribution of the general aid grant . . . 1903-1915.
Education and schools (Scotland) IV.12

983
General divisional reports on education . . . 1889-1914.
PP: 1889-1907.
NP: 1908-1914.
Education and schools (Scotland) III.5

984
Medical treatment. Regulations . . . as to grants to school boards in respect of the medical treatment of necessitous school children . . . 1915-1918.
Education and schools (Scotland) IV.17

985
Secondary education (grants to schools). Regulations . . . 1907-1914.
Education and schools (Scotland) IV.30

986
Secondary education (Scotland). Report . . . 1893-1915.
PP: 1893-1908.
NP: 1909-1915.
Education and schools (Scotland) III.9; III.11

987
Statement showing (1) An estimate of the sums receivable by the Education (Scotland) Fund . . . and of the balance available for allocation . . . (2) the allocation of such balance . . . 1912/13-1918/19.
Education and schools (Scotland) IV.10

988
Statistical lists of grant-earning day schools and institutions, continuation classes, adult education classes and central institutions. 1877-1936/37.
Title varies: to 1918/19, Return of grant-earning day schools . . .
PP: 1877-1907.
NP: 1908-1936/37.
Education and schools (Scotland) IV.4; IV.13

989
Teachers' training. Regulations for the preliminary education, training, and certification of teachers for various grades of schools . . . 1906-1920.
Education and schools (Scotland) IV.35

990
Technical education (Scotland). Return showing the extent to which and the manner in which local authorities in Scotland have allocated and applied funds to the purposes of technical

education . . . 1890/93-1905/6.
>   *Education and schools*
>   *(Scotland) IV.12(c); IV.37*

991
Training of teachers. Report, statistics,
etc. . . . 1889-1928/30.
>   Title varies: 1889-1899, Training col-
leges. Reports . . .
>   PP: 1889-1906/7.
>   NP: 1907/8-1928/30.
>   *Education and schools*
>   *(Scotland) III.11, III.14*

Scottish Gas Board

Established under the Gas Act 1948.

992
Annual report and accounts . . . 1,
1949/50+.
>   *Gas*

Scottish Health Services Council

993
Report . . . 1949+.
>   PP: 1949-1955, in: Department of
Health for Scotland. Report . . .
>   NP: 1956+.
>   *Health (Scotland)*

Scottish Home and Health Department

Formed in 1962 by the merging of the
*Department of Health for Scotland and
the *Scottish Home Department, some
of whose functions were also transferred to the newly established *Scottish
Development Department.

994
Child care in Scotland . . . (including
remand homes and approved schools).
A report of the Secretary of State for
Scotland. 1962+.
>   For earlier reports, see: Scottish
Home Department. Children in the care
of local authorities in Scotland . . .
>   1962-1966 issued by Scottish Edu-
cation Department and extracted from

its: Education in Scotland. Report . . .
>   From 1967 these functions are trans-
ferred to Scottish Home and Health
Department, and the Report is prepared
by the Social Work Services Group.

995
Criminal statistics, Scotland. 1925+.
>   Continues, in part: Prisons Depart-
ment for Scotland. Report on the judicial statistics of Scotland.
>   An abridged summary report was
issued for 1939/45.
>   *Judicial statistics (Scotland);*
>   *Criminal statistics (Scotland)*

996
Fire services (Scotland). Report of H.M.
Inspector of Fire Services for Scotland
. . . 1948/49+.
>   1967 Report entitled: Departmental
report on the fire services for Scotland.
>   *Fire—fire services (Scotland)*

997
Health and welfare services in Scotland.
Report . . . 1962+.
>   Continues, in part: Department of
Health for Scotland. Report . . .

998
Her Majesty's Chief Inspector of Constabulary for Scotland: Report . . . 1,
1858/59+.
>   To 1964, Inspector of Constabulary
for Scotland.
>   Not issued: 1940/41-1944/45.
>   *Police, etc. (Scotland)*

999
Judicial statistics, Scotland . . . Civil judicial statistics. 1925+.
>   Continues, in part: Prisons Depart-
ment for Scotland. Report on the judicial statistics of Scotland.
>   A single report was issued for 1939/
48.
>   *Judicial statistics (Scotland);*
>   *Judicial statistics, civil (Scotland)*

1000
National Health Service (Scotland) Acts
1947 to 1961. Accounts . . . Summarised
accounts of Regional Hospital Boards . . .
for Scotland . . . 1948/49+.
>   *Health (Scotland)*

1001

Prisons in Scotland. Report . . . 1939/
48+.

Continues: Prisons Department for
Scotland. Annual report . . .

Prisons (Scotland)

Scottish Home Department

Established in 1939 with a wide range of
responsibilities similar to the functions
of the *Home Office in England. In
1962 it was merged with the *Department of Health for Scotland to form the
*Scottish Home and Health Department,
some of its functions also being transferred to the newly established *Scottish
Development Department.

1003

Children in the care of local authorities
in Scotland . . . Particulars of the number
of children in care under the Children
Act 1948 . . . 1957-1958.

Later, see: Scottish Home and Health
Department. Child care in Scotland . . .

Children and young persons (Scotland)

**Scottish Hospital Endowments
Research Trust**

Under the Hospital Endowments (Scotland) Act 1953, the Trust was created to
provide schemes for the management of
endowments received by hospitals with
the National Health Service administration in Scotland.

1004

Annual report and accounts . . . 1, 1954/
55+.

Hospitals (Scotland)

Scottish Land Court

Set up in 1912 under the Small Landholders (Scotland) Act 1911, replacing
the *Crofters' Commission. Its principal
functions are to encourage the formation of small agricultural holdings and to
handle registrations of new landholders.

1005

Report as to proceedings under the
Agriculture (Scotland) Act 1948, Agricultural Holdings (Scotland) Act 1949,
Agricultural Act 1958, Small Landholders (Scotland) Acts 1886 to 1931,
and Crofters (Scotland) Acts 1955 and
1961. 1, 1912+.

Title varies: Report as to proceedings
under the Small Landholders (Scotland)
Acts 1886-1911.

Continues: Crofters' Commission. Report . . .

1940/49 covered by a single report.

Land, etc. (Scotland)

Scottish Office

The first Secretary for Scotland was appointed in 1885, and the Office assumed
a wide range of responsibilities for
Scottish affairs previously administered
by the Home Office and other agencies.
In 1926 the increasing importance of the
Office was recognized by the raising of
the Secretary's status to that of Secretary of State. He is directly responsible for the four principal Scottish
Departments, each administered by a
Secretary: the *Department of Agriculture and Fisheries for Scotland, the
*Scottish Development Department, the
*Scottish Education Department, and
the *Scottish Home and Health Department.

1006

Annual local taxation returns . . . 1880/
81-1934/35.

Title varies: 1880/81-1887/88, Abstract of returns and expenditure . . .

1880/81-1915/16, issued by Local
Government Board for Scotland.

PP: 1880/81-1915/16.

NP: 1916/17-1934/35.

Local taxation (Scotland) III.2; II.1

1007

Local Taxation (Scotland) Account. Re-

turn of payments into and out of the Local Taxation Account . . . 1896/97-1929/30.
To 1915/16, issued by Local Government Board for Scotland.
PP: 1896/97-1919/20.
NP: 1920/21-1929/30.
Local taxation (Scotland) III.4(b);
11.4

1008
New Towns (Scotland) Act 1968. Reports of the . . . Development Corporations . . . 1947/49+.
Until 1966/67, presented pursuant to the New Towns Act 1946.
Town and country planning III.2;
New towns III

1009
Private Legislation Procedure (Scotland) Act 1899. Return of all the draft provisional orders . . . 1901/2-1921.
Bills, private (Scotland)

Scottish War Savings Committee

1010
Annual report . . . 1-2, 1916/17-1917/18.
Later, see: Scottish Savings Committee. Annual report . . . 1924/25-1930/31 (NP).
War, 1914-1918 III.5

Shipbuilding Industry Board

Established in August 1966, in anticipation of enabling legislation provided by the Shipbuilding Industry Act 1967, to ascertain what changes were necessary in organization, methods of production, etc., to make the United Kingdom shipbuilding industry competitive in world markets.

1011
Report and accounts . . . 1, 1966/68+.

Shipbuilding Industry Training Board

Board established November 1964 under

Industrial Training Act 1964.

1012
Report and statement of accounts . . . 1964/65+.

Social Science Research Council

Established December 1965 under the Science and Technology Act, to encourage, support, and carry out research in the social sciences.

1013
Report . . . 1965/66+.

South East Scotland Electricity Board

Established under the Electricity Act 1947. Under the Electricity Reorganisation (Scotland) Act 1954, its functions and those of the *South West Scotland Electricity Board were taken over by the *South of Scotland Electricity Board.

1014
Report and statement of accounts . . . 1948/49-1954/55.
Electricity (Scotland)

South Eastern Electricity Board

Established under the Electricity Act 1947.

1015
Report and accounts . . . 1, 1948/49+.
Electricity

South Eastern Gas Board

Established under the Gas Act 1948.

1016
Annual report and accounts . . . 1, 1949/50+.
Gas

South of Scotland Electricity Board

Established under the Electricity Re-organisation (Scotland) Act 1954, replacing the *South East Scotland Electricity Board and the *South West Scotland Electricity Board.

1017
Annual report and accounts . . . 1955+.
Electricity (Scotland)

South Wales Electricity Board

Established under the Electricity Act 1947.

1018
Report and accounts . . . 1, 1948/49+.
Electricity

South West Scotland Electricity Board

Established under the Electricity Act 1947. Under the Electricity Reorganisation (Scotland) Act 1954, its functions and those of the *South East Scotland Electricity Board were taken over by the *South of Scotland Electricity Board.

1019
Report and statement of accounts . . . 1-7, 1948/49-1954/55.
Electricity (Scotland)

South Western Electricity Board

Established under the Electricity Act 1947.

1020
Report and accounts . . . 1, 1948/49+.
Electricity

South Western Gas Board

Established under the Gas Act 1948.

1021
Annual report and accounts . . . 1, 1948/50+.
Gas

Southern Electricity Board

Established under the Electricity Act 1947.

1022
Report and accounts . . . 1, 1948/49+.
Electricity

Southern Gas Board

Established under the Gas Act 1948.

1023
Annual report and accounts . . . 1, 1949/50+.
Gas

Spindles Board

1024
Cotton Spinning Industry Act 1936. Annual report of the Spindles Board. 1936/37-1938/39.
Cotton industry

1025
Cotton Spinning Industry Act 1936. Spindles Board. Accounts . . . 1936/37-1941.
Cotton industry

Stationery Office

Set up in 1786 under the Administrative Reform Act 1782, to provide economies by the central purchasing of supplies for government departments. During the nineteenth century its functions were gradually extended to include the printing, publishing, and sale of government publications.

1026
Report of the Controller of H.M. Stationery Office. 1-4, 1881-1904.
   Irregular.
   No more issued.
Stationery and printing;
Stationery Office

Sugar Board

Established by the Sugar Act 1956, to carry out the Government's contractual obligation to purchase sugar from producers under the Commonwealth Sugar Agreement of 1951.

1027
Report and accounts . . . 1956/58+.
Sugar

**Supreme Court of Judicature,
Northern Ireland**

1028
Land purchase. Account of H.M. High Court of Justice in Northern Ireland in respect of the functions transferred under the Northern Ireland Land Purchase (Winding Up) Act 1935 . . . 1937/38+.
   Continues: Land Purchase Commission, Northern Ireland. Accounts . . .
Land, etc. (Ireland) IV.1

**Teddington. National Physical
Laboratory**

1029
Accounts of receipts and expenditures . . . 1900/6-1915/16.
   Continued in: Exchequer and Audit Department. Trading accounts . . .
National Physical Laboratory

Thames Conservancy Office

1030
General report of the Conservators of the river Thames . . . with a statement of the accounts . . . 1857/58-1925.

Later reports not issued as government publications.
Thames

Trade Commissioner for Australia

1031
Trade of Australia. Report to the Board of Trade on the trade of the Commonwealth of Australia . . . 1911-1919.
   Continued in: Board of Trade. Department of Overseas Trade. Report on the economic and financial conditions . . .
   Not issued: 1912.
Australia

**Trade Commissioner for Dominion
of Canada and Newfoundland**

1032
Report to Board of Trade. 1906/10-1919.
   Continued in: Board of Trade. Department of Overseas Trade. Report on the economic and financial conditions . . .
Canada

Trade Commissioner for New Zealand

1033
Trade of New Zealand. Report to the Board of Trade on the trade of the Dominion of New Zealand . . . 1911-1918/20.
   Continued in: Board of Trade. Department of Overseas Trade. Report on the economic and financial conditions . . .
New Zealand

Trade Commissioner for South Africa

1034
Trade of British South Africa. Report to the Board of Trade on the trade of British South Africa . . . 1911-1919.
   Continued in: Board of Trade. Department of Overseas Trade. Report on the economic and financial conditions . . .
Africa, South

Tramp Shipping Administrative Committee

1035
Report. 1-6, 1935-1937.
  Title varies: 1-3, Interim report.
Shipping II.3

Transport Holding Company

Established under the Transport Act 1962, to hold and manage securities vested in it by the Act and to oversee and operate nationally owned road haulage, bus, shipping, and tourist companies. The Company was dismembered at the end of 1968.

1036
Annual report and accounts. 1963-1968.

Transport Users' Consultative Committee for Scotland

Established under Transport Act 1947.

1037
Annual report . . . 4, 1953+.
  Not issued: 1-3.
Transport (Scotland)

Transport Users' Consultative Committee for Wales and Monmouthshire

Established under Transport Act 1953

1038
Annual report . . . 1953+.
Transport (Wales)

Treasury

The Treasury controls the management, collection, and expenditure of the public revenue; is responsible for administering the Civil Service; and exercises general supervision over all the public departments. The origins of its present organization date from 1667, when King Charles II appointed a Treasury Commission independent of the Privy Council. Since the eighteenth century the office of the First Lord of the Treasury is usually held by the Prime Minister, while the Chancellor of the Exchequer is the effective political head of the Treasury.

1039
Accounts of the Administrator of Bulgarian property in the United Kingdom, Channel Islands and the Isle of Man . . . 1948/57+.
Bulgaria

1040
Accounts of the Administrator of Hungarian property in the United Kingdom, Channel Islands and the Isle of Man . . . 1948/57+.
Hungary

1041
Accounts of the Administrator of Roumanian property in the United Kingdom, Channel Islands and the Isle of Man . . . 1948/57+.
Roumania

1042
Air Corporations Act 1967. Statement of guarantee given by the Treasury . . . on loans proposed to be raised by the British European Airways Corporation. 1948+.
  1948 Statement issued under Civil Aviation Act 1946; 1949-1967 under Air Corporations Act 1949.
Air V.9; Aviation, civil III

1043
Air Corporations Act 1949. Statement of guarantee given by the Treasury . . . on loans proposed to be raised by the British Overseas Airways Corporation. 1940+.
  1940-1948 issued under the British Overseas Airways Act 1939.
Air V.10, 11; Aviation, civil III

1044
Air Corporations Act 1949. Statement of guarantee given by the Treasury . . . on stock issued by the British European Airways Corporation. 1949-1952.

1949 Statement issued under Civil Aviation Act 1946.
Air V.9; Aviation, civil III

1045
Air Corporations Act 1949. Statement of guarantee given by the Treasury . . . on stock issued by the British Overseas Airways Corporation. 1949-1955.
1949 Statement issued under the British Overseas Airways Act 1939.
Air V.11; Aviation, civil III

1046
Airports Authority Act 1965. Statement of guarantee given by the Treasury . . . on loans proposed to be raised by the British Airports Authority. 1965+.

1047
Analysis of the sources of war finance, and estimates of national income and expenditure . . . 1938/40-1938/44.
Continued by its: National income and expenditure . . .
Finance III.54

1048
Bank of England. Applications made by the First Lord of the Treasury and the Chancellor of the Exchequer to the Bank of England for advances to government . . . 1801-1925/26.
Bank of England

1049
Borrowing (Control and Guarantees) Act 1946. Statement of guarantee given by the Treasury . . . in respect of advances by the Bank of England for the purpose of providing temporary financial assistance for the Fairfield Shipbuilding and Engineering Company Limited and Fairfield Rowan Limited. 1965+.

1050
Channel Islands (Crown rights). Return of revenues . . . 1881/82-1909/16.
Irregular.
Channel Islands

1051
Civil Aviation Act 1946. Statement of guarantee given by the Treasury . . . on loans proposed to be raised by the British South American Airways Corporation. 1948.
No more issued. The Corporation was merged with British Overseas Airways Corporation in 1949.
Air V.12

1052
Civil Aviation Act 1946. Statement of guarantee given by the Treasury . . . on stock issued by the British South American Airways Corporation. 1949.
No more issued. The Corporation was merged with British Overseas Airways Corporation in 1949.
Air V.12

1053
Civil estimates . . . 1890/91+.
Continues, in part, its: Civil Services and Revenue Departments. Estimates . . .
From 1890/91-1961/62, its Revenue Departments. Estimates . . . are issued separately. From 1962/63, they are included in Class I of the Civil estimates.
Civil Service IV.1

1054
Civil estimates . . . Supplementary estimates . . . 1852/53+.
Title varies.
Civil Service IV.5; IV.9

1055
Civil List pensions. List of all pensions . . . charged upon the Civil List. 1830-1939/40.
Civil List pensions; Civil List

1056
Civil servants (retirement at 65). Treasury minute . . . stating the circumstances under which certain civil servants have been retained in the service after they have attained the age of sixty-five . . . 1892-1915.
Civil Service V.22; V.20

1057
Civil staffs employed in government departments. Statement . . . 1914/19-1960.
Frequency varies.
Not issued: 1939-1944.
Civil Service V.23

1058
Coal Act 1938. Statement of guarantee given by the Treasury . . . on loans proposed to be raised by the Coal Commission. 1938/39-1943/44.
Coal industry IV.15

1059
Coal Industry Nationalisation Act 1946. Statement of guarantee given by the Treasury . . . on loans proposed to be raised by the National Coal Board. 1964+.

1060
Colonial Loans Acts 1949, 1952 and 1962. Statement of guarantee given by the Treasury . . . on loans to be made . . . by the International Bank for Reconstruction and Development. 1952+.
Colonies III

1061
Colonial Loans Acts 1949 and 1952. Statement of the total sums issued out of the Consolidated Fund . . . in fulfilment of guarantees given by the Treasury . . . 1966/67+.

1062
Colonial Stock Acts 1877 to 1934. Copy of Treasury list of colonial stocks in respect of which the provisions of the Act are for the time being complied with . . . 1911-1938.
Colonies III.8

1063
Crown's Nominee Account . . . Abstract account . . . 1877+.
PP: 1877-1920.
NP: 1921+.
Not issued: 1938-1944.
Crown's Nominee; Crown Nominee

1064
Currency and Bank Notes Act 1954. Copy of Treasury minute . . . relative to the fiduciary note issue . . . 1931+.
To 1954, under 1928 Act.
Irregular.
Currency and coinage

1065
Cyprus. Revenues, sums paid, etc. (Turkish Loan). Return of all sums paid . . . 1878/79-1909/12.
Irregular.
Cyprus

1066
Debts Clearing Offices and Import Restrictions Act 1934. Accounts of the Anglo-Spanish, Anglo-Roumanian, Anglo-Italian, and Anglo-Turkish Clearing Offices . . . 1935/36-1948/49.
1935/36, Anglo-Spanish Clearing Office only.
Debts and debtors

1067
Disabled persons in government employment. Statement . . . 1946/47-1960.
Civil Service V.8

1068
Duchy of Cornwall. An account of the receipts and disbursements. 1841/42-1921.
Preceded by its: Duchies of Cornwall and Lancaster. Revenues . . . 1837/38-1841/42.
PP: 1841/42-1920.
NP: 1921.
Cornwall, Duchy of

1069
Duchy of Lancaster. Account of the receipts and disbursements. 1850/51-1921.
Preceded by its: Duchies of Cornwall and Lancaster. Revenues . . . 1837/38-1841/42.
PP: 1850/51-1920.
NP: 1921.
Lancaster, Duchy of

1070
Economic survey. 1947-1962.
Economy; Economic survey

1071
Electricity Act 1947. Statement of guarantee given by the Treasury . . . on loans proposed to be raised by the Central Electricity Authority. 1948-1957.
1948-1954 as British Electricity Authority.
Later, see its: Electricity Act 1957. Statement . . . Electricity Council.
Electricity

1072
Electricity Act 1947. Statement of guarantee given by the Treasury . . . on stock issued by the British Electricity Authority. 1948-1955.
Electricity

1073
Electricity Act 1957. Statement of guarantee given by the Treasury . . . on loans proposed to be raised by the Electricity Council. 1957+.

Earlier, see its: Electricity Act 1947. Statement . . . Central Electricity Authority.

Electricity

1074
Estimates . . . Memorandum by the Financial Secretary to the Treasury. 1962/63+.

Earlier (1950/51-1961/62), Memorandum was included in its: Civil estimates . . . ; and its: Revenue Departments. Estimates . . .

1075
Estimates. Revenue Departments. Appendix. Post Office. Details of salaries, wages, and allowances in the London Postal Service (subhead A), and at provincial post offices in the United Kingdom (subhead C) . . . 1910/11-1920/21.

Civil Service IV.6

1076
Estimates. Revenue Departments. Post Office. Details of postal and telegraph subheads referred to in the Revenue Departments estimate . . . 1871/72-1909/10.

Issued as an Appendix to its: Revenue Departments. Estimates . . .

Civil Service IV.1; IV.6

1077
Ex-service men employed in government offices. Statement . . . 1919/20-1938.

Frequency varies.

Civil Service V.9

1078
External debt. Return . . . 1919/20-1919/22.

National Debt II.3

1079
Finance accounts of the United Kingdom . . . 1817/18+.

Preceded by its: Annual class accounts . . . , issued separately for Great Britain and for Ireland.

Finance; Finance accounts; Finance III.1

1080
Finance Act 1934. Account . . . of sums issued out of the Consolidated Fund in fulfilment of guarantees given under

Section 25 of the Act. 1934/35-1959/60.

Title varies: 1934/35-1941/42, Finance Act 1934. Statement of conversion loans guaranteed by the Treasury . . . and Account . . .

1940/41 issued in its: Trade Facilities Acts 1921 to 1926; and its: Finance Act 1934 . . . Statement . . .

Finance IV.24; III.23

1081
Financial relations. Statement of the financial position between the British government and the government of the Irish Free State . . . 1923/24-1925/26.

Ireland III.10

1082
Financial statement. Copy of statement of revenue and expenditure . . . 1880+.

1083
Gas Act 1948. Statement of guarantee given by the Treasury . . . on loans proposed to be raised by the Gas Council. 1949+.

Gas and water IV.4; Gas III

1084
Gas Act 1948. Statement of guarantee given by the Treasury . . . on stock issued by the Gas Council. 1949-1955.

Gas and water IV.7; Gas III

1085
German Reparation (Recovery) Act 1921. Statement . . . 1921/22-1924/25.

Germany III.28

1086
Government departments (contracts). Return . . . 1879/86-1912/13.

Contracts and contractors (government)

1087
Government departments securities. Return . . . 1879-1915.

Government department securities; Government

1088
Government expenditure below the line. 1958/62-1964/65.

Continued by its: Loans from the Consolidated Fund.

1089
Government information services. Statement showing the estimated expenditure ... 1950/51-1956/57.
Information

1090
Greek Loan, 1832. Account ... 1843-1939.
Irregular.
Not issued: 1916-1918, 1921-1933.
Greece

1091
Greek Loan of 1898. Account ... 1898/99+.
Irregular.
Greece

1092
Housing Act 1914. Account ... 1914/15-1962/63.
PP: 1914/15-1939/40; 1962/63.
NP: 1940/41-1957/58.
Not issued: 1958/59-1961/62.
Housing IV.1

1093
Hydro-Electric Development (Scotland) Act 1943. Statement of guarantee given by the Treasury . . . on loans proposed to be raised by the North of Scotland Hydro-Electric Board. 1945/46+.
Electricity (Scotland)

1094
Hydro-Electric Development (Scotland) Act 1943. Statement of guarantee given by the Treasury . . . on loans proposed to be raised by the South of Scotland Electricity Board. 1955+.
Electricity (Scotland)

1095
Imperial Defence Act 1888. Account of all moneys issued from the Consolidated Fund, of sums borrowed, and of transactions ... in pursuance of the Imperial Defence Act 1888. 1888/90-1900/1.
Imperial and naval defence;
Imperial defence

1096
Imperial Ottoman Loan of 1855. Account ... 1878/79-1962/63.
Irregular.
Turkey

1097
Imperial revenue (collection and expenditure) (Great Britain and Ireland). Return ... 1819/96-1920/21.
Revenue III.10;
Revenue and expenditure II.4

1098
Internal debt. Return ... 1921-1922.
National Debt II.5

1099
Iron and Steel Act 1949. Statement of guarantee given by the Treasury . . . on loans proposed to be raised by the Iron and Steel Corporation of Great Britain ... 1950-1953.
Iron and steel

1100
Iron and Steel Act 1949. Statement of guarantee given by the Treasury . . . on stock issued by the Iron and Steel Corporation. 1951-1952.
Iron and steel

1101
Iron and Steel Act 1967. Statement of guarantee given by the Treasury ... on loans proposed to be raised by the British Steel Corporation. 1967+.

1102
Loans from the Consolidated Fund. 1965/66-1967/68.
Continues its: Government expenditure below the line.
Continued by its: Loans from the National Loans Fund.

1103
Loans from the National Loans Fund. 1968/69+.
Continues its: Loans from the Consolidated Fund.

1104
London County Council. Returns relating to the Council ... 1889-1911/12.
London IV.7; IV.11

1105
Memorandum on present and pre-war expenditure ... 1920/21-1925/26.
Civil Service V.6

1106
National Debt. Return showing for ...

each financial year . . . (1) the total amount of dead weight debt outstanding . . . (2) a similar statement in respect of other capital liabilities (3) a similar statement in respect of the aggregate gross liabilities of the State . . . 1908-1930/31.

National Debt II.2

1107
National Debt return. 1835/89+.
Title varies: Liabilities, assets, and expenditure. Return . . . ; and: National Debt. Return showing (1) the capital liabilities of the State . . . and (2) the gross and net expenditure charged annually. Short title only used from 1964/65.
Issued in abridged form 1940/41-1945/46: National Debt: Return showing transactions connected with the National Debt . . .

National Debt III.7; II.7, 8

1108
National Health Service Act 1966. Statement of guarantee given by the Treasury . . . in respect of advances by Messrs. Glyn Mills & Company for the purposes of providing temporary financial assistance for the General Practice Finance Corporation. 1966+.

1109
National Health Service Act 1966. Statement of guarantee given by the Treasury . . . on stock issued by the General Practice Finance Corporation. 1968+.

1110
National income and expenditure of the United Kingdom . . . 1938/45-1946/50.
Continues its: Analysis of the sources of war finance . . .
Continued, in reduced form, by its: Preliminary estimates of national income and balance of payments . . .

Income and expenditure, private; National income

1111
National Loans Fund. Statement of assets and liabilities . . . 1968+.

1112
Pacific Cable Act 1901. Account . . . 1901/2-1926/27.

Later, see: Pacific Cable Board. Pacific Cable Act 1927. Report and accounts . . . 1927/28. (NP)
PP: 1901/2-1920/21.
NP: 1921/22-1926/27.

Telegraphs and telephones IV.11

1113
Permanent charges commutation. Return . . . 1891-1915/25.

Consolidated Fund

1114
Post Office Act 1961. Statement of guarantee given by the Treasury . . . on loans proposed to be raised by the Postmaster General. 1961+.

1115
Post Office Fund. Statement showing the net surplus . . . 1933/34-1939/40.

Post Office IV.32

1116
Post Office (revenue and expenditure). Return of revenue and expenditure for each year from 1869/70, and an estimate of the same for the year . . . 1890/91-1901/2.
Title varies.

Post Office IV.1

1117
Post Office Savings Bank investment accounts . . . 1966+.

1118
Post Office Savings Banks. An account of all deposits received and paid . . . 1861+.
PP: 1861-1920.
NP: 1921+.

Savings banks IV.5; IV.4

1119
Post Office telegraphs. Account showing the gross amount received and expended on account of the telegraph service . . . and the balance of the receipts over the expenditure . . . 1875/76-1908/9.

Telegraphs IV.2; Telegraphs and telephones IV.1

1120
Post Office telegraphs (revenue and expenditure). Return of revenue and expenditure of the Post Office telegraphs for each year from 1869/70 . . . and an

estimate . . . 1890/91-1901/2.
Telegraphs IV.2; Telegraphs and telephones IV.1

1121
Preliminary estimates of national income and balance of payments. 1948/51+.

For earlier, more detailed survey, see its: National income and expenditure of the United Kingdom . . .
National income

1122
Public accounts. Defence (Air) Votes. Copy of Treasury Minute . . . authorising the temporary application of surpluses on certain Defence (Air) Votes . . . to meet deficits on other Defence (Air) Votes for the same year. 1919/20+.

Title varies: . . . temporary application of excesses . . . (used in years when the sum will be insufficient to cover the deficit and an additional Vote will be required).

Until 1932/33 these Minutes serve either of two purposes: (1) to indicate expectation of deficiency and authorization of virement, or (2) to give fuller details of virement already authorized by an earlier Minute. From 1933/34, the first of these purposes is served by a Minute using the wording . . . *regarding* the temporary application of surpluses . . .
Air IV.6; Air Force III

1123
Public Accounts. Defence (Air) Votes. Copy of Treasury Minute . . . regarding the application of surpluses on certain Air Votes . . . to meet deficits on other Air Votes. 1933/34+.

Title varies.

For earlier Minutes in this series, see no. 1122.

Not issued: 1939/40-1945/46.
Air IV.6: Air Force III

1124
Public Accounts. Defence (Army) Votes. Copy of Treasury Minute . . . authorising the temporary application of surpluses on certain Defence (Army) Votes . . . to meet deficits on other Defence (Army) Votes for the same year. 1888/89+.

Title varies.
See note under no. 1122.
Army IV.13

1125
Public Accounts. Defence (Army) Votes. Copy of Treasury Minute . . . regarding the application of surpluses on certain Army Votes . . . to meet deficits on other Army Votes. 1933/34+.

Title varies.

For earlier Minutes in this series, see no. 1124 and note under no. 1122.

Not issued: 1939/40-1945/46.
Army IV.13

1126
Public Accounts. Defence (Navy) Votes. Copy of Treasury Minute . . . authorising the temporary application of surpluses on certain Defence (Navy) Votes . . . to meet deficits on other Defence (Navy) Votes for the same year. 1888/89+.

Title varies.
See note under no. 1122.
Navy IV.11

1127
Public Accounts. Defence (Navy) Votes. Copy of Treasury Minute . . . regarding the application of surpluses on certain Navy Votes . . . to meet deficits on other Navy Votes. 1933/34+.

Title varies.

For earlier Minutes in this series, see no. 1126 and note under no. 1122.

Not issued: 1939/40-1945/46.
Navy IV.11

1128
Public boards. List of members of public boards of a commercial character . . . 1950+.
Boards, public

1128a
Public expenditure . . . 1963/68+.

1129
Public income and expenditure . . . An account . . . 1856/57+.
Income and expenditure, public 2; Revenue and expenditure II.5; Finance accounts

1130
Public income and expenditure (net).

Return of net public income and net public expenditure . . . 1875/85-1893/1908.
> *Income and expenditure, public 6:*
> *Revenue and expenditure II.6*

1131
Public revenue (interception). . . Return . . . 1895/96-1911/14.
> *Revenue III.11;*
> *Revenue and expenditure II.10*

1132
Public social services (total expenditure . . .). Return . . . 1918-1937.
> *Revenue and expenditure II.2*

1133
Public Works Loan Bill . . . Statement . . . 1900-1927.
> *Works, public*

1134
Revenue and expenditure (England, Scotland, and Ireland). Return . . . 1891/92-1933/34.
> 1931/32-1933/34, England and Scotland only.
> Not issued: 1921/22-1930/31.
> *Financial relations III.2;*
> *Revenue and expenditure II.12*

1135
Revenue (collection of taxes). Return . . . 1898/1900-1912/14.
> *Revenue and expenditure II.11*

1136
Revenue Departments. Estimates . . . 1890/91-1961/62.
> Continues, in part, its: Civil Services and Revenue Departments. Estimates . . .
> From 1962/63, estimates for Revenue Departments are included in Class I of its: Civil estimates . . .
> *Civil Service IV.1; IV.6;*
> *Civil estimates*

1137
Sardinian Loan. Account of the sums issued out of the Consolidated Fund and advanced to the King of Sardinia . . . 1855-1902.
> *Sardinia; Sardinian loan*

1138
Savings banks. Return from each savings bank in England and Wales, Scotland and Ireland . . . 1852-1919/20.
> Title varies: Trustee savings banks . . .
> *Savings banks IV.1; IV.8*

1139
Savings Banks Funds: Post Office Savings Banks Fund. Account . . . showing the interest accrued in respect of the securities standing in the names of the National Debt Commissioners . . . 1878/79-1966.
> Continued in two series, its: Trustee Savings Banks Acts 1954 to 1968. Fund for the Banks for Savings. Accounts . . . (PP); and its: Post Office Savings Banks Fund. An account . . . showing the interest accrued . . . (NP).
> PP: 1878/79-1920.
> NP: 1921-1966.
> *Savings banks IV.2(c); IV.9*

1140
Septennial actuarial report on the assets and liabilities of the Elementary School Teachers' Deferred Annuity Fund. 1-2, 1899/1906-1907/13.
> *Education and schools IV.92*

1141
Statement of excesses. Civil estimates. Statement of the sum required to be voted to make good excesses on certain grants for civil services. 1864/65+.
> *Civil Service IV.10; IV.5;*
> *Civil estimates*

1142
Statement relating to length of service of temporary clerical and typing staffs employed in government departments . . . April 1935-April 1938.
> *Civil Service V.27*

1143
Superannuation Act 1887. Return . . . of the Army and Navy officers permitted . . . to hold civil employment . . . 1887/88-1913/14.
> *Civil Service V.7; Army V.30*

1144
Supreme Court: Prize, etc., Deposit Account (1914-1918 War). Account of the receipts and payments of the Accounting Officer of the Vote for the Supreme Court on behalf of the Admiralty Divi-

sion in Prize . . . 1914/15-1930/55.
Courts of law IV.11

1145
Supreme Court: Prize, etc., Deposit Account (1939-1945 War). Account of the receipts and payments of the Accounting Officer of the Vote for the Supreme Court on behalf of the Admiralty Division in Prize . . . 1939/42-1939/55.
Courts of law IV.11

1146
Taxes and imposts (rates, receipts, produce, etc.). Return . . . 1865/66-1920/21.
Not issued: 1914/15-1917/18.
Revenue and expenditure III.15; II.13

1147
Teachers' Pension Fund (Ireland). Return . . . 1902-March 1922.
Education and schools (Ireland) III.18

1148
Trade Facilities Acts. Guarantees which the Treasury have stated their willingness to give . . . Jan./March 1922-Oct./Dec. 1926.
Trade IV.55

1149
Trade Facilities Acts 1921 to 1926. Account . . . of the total sums issued from the Consolidated Fund in fulfilment of guarantees given under the Acts . . . 1942/43-1961/62.
Continues its: Trade Facilities Acts 1921 to 1926, and Finance Act 1934 . . . Statement . . .
Trade IV.55

1150
Trade Facilities Acts 1921 to 1926. I. Statement of guarantees which the Treasury have given to completion of the scheme on March 31, 1927. II. Account . . . of the total sums issued from the Consolidated Fund in fulfilment of guarantees . . . 1926/27-1934/35.
Continued by its: Trade Facilities Acts 1921 to 1926, and Finance Act 1934 . . . Statement . . .
Trade IV.55

1151
Trade Facilities Acts 1921 to 1926, and Finance Act 1934. Trade Facilities Acts.

I. Statement of guarantees which the Treasury have given to completion of the scheme on 31st March, 1927. II. Account . . . of the total sums issued from the Consolidated Fund in fulfilment of guarantees. Finance Act 1934. I. Statement of conversion loans . . . II. Account . . . of any sums issued out of the Consolidated Fund . . . 1935/36-1941/42.
Continues its: Trade Facilities Acts 1921 to 1926. I. Statement . . .
Continued by its: Trade Facilities Acts 1921 to 1926. Account . . .
Trade IV.55

1152
Transport Act 1947. Statement of guarantee given by the Treasury . . . on loans proposed to be raised by the British Transport Commission. 1956-1962.
Transport

1153
Transport Act 1947. Statement of guarantee given by the Treasury . . . on stock issued by the British Transport Commission. 1948-1957.
Transport

1154
Transport Act 1962. Statement of guarantee given by the Treasury . . . on loans proposed to be raised by the British Railways Board. 1962+.

1155
Transport Act 1962. Statement of guarantee given by the Treasury . . . on loans proposed to be raised by the British Transport Docks Board. 1962+.

1156
Transport Act 1962. Statement of guarantee given by the Treasury . . . on loans proposed to be raised by the British Waterways Board. 1962+.

1157
Transport Act 1962. Statement of guarantee given by the Treasury . . . on loans proposed to be raised by the London Transport Board. 1962+.

1158
Transport Act 1962. Statement of guarantee given by the Treasury . . . on loans

proposed to be raised by the Transport Holding Company. 1962+.

1159
Treasury Chest Fund . . . An account . . . 1847/48-1957/58.
Title varies: 1847/48-1854/55, Commissariat Chest account.
Treasury Chest

1160
Trustee Savings Banks Acts 1954 to 1968. Fund for the Banks for Savings. Accounts . . . 1966/67+.
Continues its: Trustee Savings Banks. Account . . . (NP); and, in part, its: Savings Banks Funds: Post Office Savings Banks Fund. Account . . .

1161
Vote on account . . . Civil estimates and Defence (Central) estimate . . . 1857/58+.
Title varies.
Civil Service V.15; IV.11;
Civil estimates

1162
Votes of credit. Statement of services to be provided for . . . 1940/41-1945/46.
Finance III.50

1163
War damage. Statement of the payments by the War Damage Commission . . . 1941/42-1945/46.
War damage

1164
War Pensions, etc., Statutory Committee. Copy of accounts . . . 1916/17.
No more issued.
Pensions (naval and military and
Air Force) III.3

Trustee Savings Banks
Inspection Committee

1165
Annual report. 1, 1891/92+.
PP: 1-29, 1891/92-1919/20.
NP: 30, 1920/21+.
Savings banks III

Unemployment Assistance Board

Established by the Unemployment Assistance Act 1934. In 1944 it became the Assistance Board and in 1948, with greatly increased responsibilities, the *National Assistance Board.

1167
Report . . . 1935-1938.
Unemployment III.5

Unemployment Insurance
Statutory Committee

1168
Unemployment Insurance Acts 1935 to 1944. Reports of the Unemployment Insurance Statutory Committee . . . on the financial condition of the Unemployment Fund. 1934-1947.
Insurance,
National Unemployment III.11

United Kingdom Atomic
Energy Authority

Established August 1954 by the Atomic Energy Authority Act, taking over responsibility for atomic energy from the Ministry of Supply.

1169
Atomic Energy Authority Act 1954. Report and accounts of the United Kingdom Atomic Energy Authority . . . 1, 1954/55+.
Accounts were issued separately to 1964/65 by Exchequer and Audit Department.
Atomic energy

United Kingdom Delegation
to the Unesco General Conference

1170
Report on the . . . General Conference of the United Nations Educational, Scientific and Cultural Organisation. 3rd-11th

sessions, 1949-1960.

For a Report on the 2nd Conference, 1947, see: Ministry of Education. UNESCO. Documents relating to the 2nd session of the General Conference ... (NP)

Not issued: 1-2, 9-10.

Treaties III.21; United Nations

University Grants Committee

Set up by Treasury Minute, July 1919, assuming powers relating to university grants from the *Board of Education and the *Scottish Education Department.

1171
Annual survey ... 1963/64+.

Earlier, issued as preface to its: Returns ... 1958/59-1961/62.

1172
Report ... 1920/21-1934/35.

Title varies: 1921/22-1922/23, Returns ... ; 1923/24-1934/35, Report, including returns ...

Later, see its: Returns ...

PP: 1920/21.

NP: 1921/22-1934/35.

Universities and colleges III.3

1173
Returns from universities and university colleges in receipt of Exchequer grant ... 1919/20+.

1923/24-1934/35 issued in its: Report, including returns ...

PP: 1919/20; 1949/50+.

NP: 1920/21-1948/49.

Not issued: 1939/40-1946/47.

Universities and colleges IV.6

1174
University development. Interim report ... 1947/51+.

Each report covers a four-year period, immediately preceding its: University development. Report ...

1962/66 issued in its: Annual survey ... 1965/66.

Universities and colleges

1175
University development. Report by the University Grants Committee. 1, 1919/21+.

Normally quinquennial.

PP: 6, 1947/52+.

NP: 1-5, 1919/21-1935/47.

Universities and colleges

Wales Gas Board

Established under the Gas Act 1948.

1176
Annual report and accounts ... 1, 1949/50+.

Gas

War Cabinet

1177
Report. 1917-1918.

War, 1914-1918 III.6

War Office

The War Office, responsible for the Army, has been subject to many reorganizations. The Office developed gradually in importance until a Secretary of State was appointed in 1794. For the first part of the nineteenth century this Secretary was also responsible for the colonies, and it was not until 1854 that these duties were separated. The Defence (Transfer of Functions) Act 1964 consolidated the administration of the three fighting Services under the *Ministry of Defence.

1178
Annual return of the Territorial Force. 1908-1919/20.

Return continued in its: General annual report on the British Army ...

PP: 1908-1913.

NP: 1919/20.

Not issued: 1914/18.

Army V.44

1179
Army estimates ... 1801-1963/64.

From 1964/65 incorporated in: Min-

istry of Defence. Defence estimates . . .
Army 21; IV.1

1180
Army estimates. Supplementary estimates . . . 1854-1962/63.
From 1963/64 see: Ministry of Defence. Army Department. Supplementary
estimate. Defence (Army).
Army IV.4; IV.10

1181
Army (Ordnance Factories). Statement
of the sum required to be voted to
make good excesses . . . 1914/15-1920/
21.
1915/16 issued by Treasury, Ordnance
·Factories at that date being controlled
by the Ministry of Munitions.
Not issued: 1916/17-1919/20.
Ordnance factories I.3

1182
Army (Royal Ordnance Factories). Sup-
plementary estimate . . . 1889/90-1938/
39.
Irregular.
Ordnance and small arms, etc. III.1;
Ordnance factories I.5

1183
Army (training of officers). Report of
the Advisory Board, London School of
Economics . . . for the training of officers
. . . 1907-1913/14.
Army III.21

1184
Barracks Act 1890. Account showing the
money raised and issued . . . 1890/91-
1901/2.
Army V.10; V.5

1185
Barracks and Military Works Acts. Approximate estimate of expenditure . . .
1889/90-1914/15.
Army IV.5

1186
General annual report on the British
Army . . . with abstracts for previous
years . . . 1872-1938.
A single Report was issued for Oct.
1913/Sept. 1919.
Army IV.3; III.1

1187
Memorandum of the Secretary of State
for War relating to the Army estimates
. . . 1887/88-1962/63.
Later included in: Ministry of Defence. Statement on the Defence estimates . . .
Not issued: 1939/40-1946/47.
Army IV.2; IV.3

1188
Military savings banks. Statement . . .
1843/44-1919/20.
Savings banks 10; IV.3(a); IV.2

1189
Military Works Act 1897 . . . Account . . .
1896/97-1915/16.
Army V.10(b); V.5

1190
Report on the discipline and management of the military prisons and deten-
tion barracks. 1848-1913.
Military prisons; Prisons III.17; II.7

1191
Royal Ordnance Factories. Estimate . . .
1888/89-1939/40; 1960/61-1962/63.
To 1887/88, Estimate was included
in: War Office. Army estimates . . .
1943/44-1959/60, in: Treasury. Civil
estimates . . .
1963/64, in: War Office. Army estimates . . .
1964/65+ in: Ministry of Defence.
Defence estimates . . .
Not issued: 1940/41-1942/43.
Ordnance and small arms, etc. III;
Ordnance factories I.1

1192
Volunteer Corps of Great Britain. An-
nual return . . . 1875-1907.
Title varies: 1875-1879, Abstract of
annual returns . . .
Volunteer Corps V.1, 9; Volunteers

1193
Vote A: Estimate of the maximum
number of men on the establishment of
the Army exclusive of India . . . 1919/
20-1922/23.
Army IV.14

1194
Vote 10, Works and Buildings. Statement of proposed expenditure out of the

Vote of Credit on new works, etc., of a permanent character . . . 1915/16-1918/19.

Army IV.16

1195
War Office purchasing (repayment) services. Estimate . . . 1960/61-1962/63.
Later, included in: Ministry of Defence. Defence estimates . . .

War Office. Army Medical Department

1196
Report on the health of the Army. 1-73, 1859-1937.
PP: 1-55, 1859-1913.
NP: 56-73, 1914, 1921-1937.
Not issued: 1915-1920.
Army III.30; III.20

War Pensions, etc. Statutory Committee

1197
Report . . . 1916.
No more issued.
Pensions (naval and military and Air Force) III.3

Water Resources Board

Established July 1964, to advise and assist river authorities in planning conservation, supply, and use of water resources.

1198
Water Resources Act, 1963. Annual report of the Water Resources Board. 1, 1964+.

Water Supply Industry Training Board

Established June 1965 under Industrial Training Act 1964.

1199
Report and statement of accounts . . . 1965/66+.

Wellington College

1200
Report of the Governors . . . 1881-1906.
Wellington College

Welsh Office

A Minister of State for Welsh Affairs was appointed in December 1957, to assist the Minister of Housing and Local Government in his functions as Minister for Welsh Affairs. In October 1964 a Secretary of State for Welsh Affairs was appointed, with Cabinet rank.

1201
Cymru: Wales. 1, 1945/46+.
Title varies: 1, 1945/46, Wales and Monmouthshire. Summary of government action; 2-18, 1946/47-1963, Wales and Monmouthshire. Report on developments and government action; 19-21, 1964-1966, Wales.
1-6, 1945/46-1950/51 issued by Ministry of Health; 7-11, 1951/52-1955/56 by Home Office; 12-13, 1956/57-1957/58 by Ministry of Housing and Local Government; 14, 1959+ by Welsh Office.
Wales

West African Currency Board

1202
Report. 1912/14-1919/20.
Later reports not issued as government publications.
Africa III.4(b)

West Midlands Gas Board

Established under the Gas Act 1948.

1203
Annual report and accounts . . . 1, 1949/50+.
Gas

White Fish Authority

Established under the Sea Fish Industry Act 1951, the Authority is the successor to the White Fish Commission set up in 1938 but suspended owing to the outbreak of war in 1939. Its primary task is to reorganize, develop, and regulate the industry.

1204
Annual report and accounts . . . 1, 1951/52+.

Fisheries III

Wool, Jute and Flax Industry Training Board

Established November 1964, under the Industrial Training Act 1964, as the Wool Industry Training Board. The present title was adopted in 1966.

1205
Report and statement of accounts . . . 1, 1964/65+.

Woolwich. Royal Military Academy

1206
Report of the Board of Visitors appointed . . . for the inspection of the Royal Military Academy, Woolwich . . . 1872-1900.

Woolwich Academy; Army III.29

Yorkshire Electricity Board

Established under the Electricity Act 1947.

1207
Report and accounts . . . 1, 1948/49+.

Electricity

Ireland

Ireland was a part of the United Kingdom from the Act of Union 1800 until the Irish Free State (Agreement) Act 1922 transformed it into a self-governing dominion. The six counties of Northern Ireland remained part of the United Kingdom, with a Parliament in Belfast as well as representation in the British Parliament. The Irish Free State in 1936 changed its name to Eire and in 1948 became the Republic of Ireland, severing its links with the British Commonwealth. Many of the publications of Irish Departments that appeared in the Parliamentary Papers until 1921 or 1922 were later continued by the governments of the Irish Free State and of Northern Ireland.

Belfast. Queen's College

1208
Report of the President . . . 1851/52-1908/9.
   Preceded by: Report of the Presidents of the Queen's Colleges in Ireland, 1849/50-1850/51.
      1910, became Queen's University.
         Universities and colleges (Ireland)

Board of National Education in Ireland

1209
Report of the Commissioners . . . 1-87, 1834-1920/21.
   PP: 1-86, 1834-1919/20.
   NP: 87, 1920/21.
   Not issued: 80, 1913/14 (but Appendices I and II were issued).
      Education II.1; Education and schools (Ireland) III.4; II.3

Board of Public Works (Ireland)

1210
Annual report of the Commissioners of Public Works in Ireland . . . 1-89, 1832/33-1920/21.
      Public works and buildings II.1; Works, public (Ireland)

Board of Superintendence of Dublin Hospitals

1211
Report . . . 1-62, 1857/58-1919/20.
         Dublin

Census Office (Ireland)

1212
Census of Ireland. 1851-1911.
Population (Ireland)

Commissioners of Charitable Donations and Bequests for Ireland

1213
Report . . . 1-75, 1845-1919.
Charities II.1; Charities (Ireland)

Commissioners of Education in Ireland

1214
Annual report . . . 1813/14-1921.
PP: 1813/14-1920.
NP: 1921.
Education II.1; Education and schools (Ireland) III.1; II.1

Congested Districts Board for Ireland

1215
Report . . . 1-30, 1891/92-1921/22.
PP: 1891-1919/20.
NP: 1920/21-1921/22.
Congested districts (Ireland)

Cork. Queen's College

1216
Report of the President . . . 1851/52-1908-9.
Preceded by: Report of the Presidents of the Queen's Colleges in Ireland, 1849/50-1850/51.
1909, became University College, Cork, part of National University of Ireland.
Universities and colleges (Ireland)

Department of Agriculture and Technical Instruction for Ireland

Established 1900. Before this date its publications were issued by various agencies, the statistical reports and returns generally coming from the *Registrar General (Ireland).

1217
Agricultural and technical instruction schemes (Ireland). Local contributions. Return . . . 1906-1914/15.
Agriculture (Ireland) III.3

1218
Agricultural prices . . . Return. 1881/1909-1881/1920.
Agriculture (Ireland) III.5

1219
Agricultural statistics, Ireland . . . General abstracts showing the acreage under crops and the number and description of livestock. 1852/53-1920.
Agriculture (Ireland) IV.3; III.6

1220
Agricultural statistics, Ireland. Report and tables relating to Irish migratory agricultural labourers. 1880-1915.
Emigration and migration (Ireland); Agriculture (Ireland) II.3

1221
Agricultural statistics, Ireland . . . Return of prices . . . 1900-1915.
Agriculture (Ireland) III.5

1222
Agricultural statistics, Ireland. Tables showing the extent in statute acres, produce of the crops, and numbers of live stock . . . 1881-1908.
Agriculture (Ireland) IV.3; III.6

1223
Agricultural statistics of Ireland . . . with detailed report . . . 1847/48-1917.
Agriculture 8; Agriculture (Ireland) IV.3; III.6

1224
Annual general report . . . 1-21, 1900/1-1920/21.
PP: 1-19, 1900/1-1918/19.
NP: 20-21, 1919/20-1920/21.
Agriculture (Ireland) II.1

1225
Annual report in regard to the Loan

Fund system of Ireland . . . 1-78, 1839-1915.
Title varies: 1-77, 1839-1914, Loan Fund Board. Annual report . . .
Loan Fund Board (Ireland);
Loans (Ireland) II; Loans III.1

1226
Banking, railway and shipping statistics, Ireland. 1885-1916/17.
Shipping statistics (for 1879/89) first added 1889/90.
Statistical tables III.16;
Banks and banking (Ireland)

1227
Report of proceedings under the Diseases of Animals Acts . . . 1882-1922.
PP: 1882-1919.
NP: 1920-1922.
Cattle, etc. (Ireland) 9; II.1

1228
Report of proceedings under the Fertilisers and Feeding Stuffs Act 1906 . . . 1908/9-1914.
A summary report for 1907/14 was also issued.
Not issued: 1913.
Fertilisers and feeding stuffs (Ireland)

1229
Report on the trade in imports and exports at Irish ports. 1-18, 1904-1921.
PP: 1904-1919.
NP: 1920-1921.
Trade IV.31

Department of Agriculture and Technical Instruction for Ireland. Fisheries Branch

1230
Report on the sea and inland fisheries . . . 1869-1921.
1869-1899, issued by Fisheries Office (Ireland).
PP: 1869-1919.
NP: 1920-1921.
Fisheries (Ireland)

Dublin. Metropolitan Police Office

1231
Statistical tables of the Dublin Metro-

politan Police. 1894-1919.
Statistical tables III.18;
Police (Ireland)

Dublin. National Gallery of Ireland

1232
Report of the Director . . . 1883-1920.
Later continued as publication of the Irish Free State.
PP: 1883-1920.
Not issued: 1916-1918.
National Gallery (Ireland)

Dublin. Royal University of Ireland

1233
Report . . . 1-27, 1882-1908.
Preceded by: Queen's University. Report . . . 1851/52-1881/82. 1909, dissolved; replaced by National University of Ireland.
Universities and colleges (Ireland)

Galway. Queen's College

1234
Report of the President . . . 1851/52-1908/9.
Preceded by: Report of the Presidents of the Queen's Colleges in Ireland, 1849/50-1850/51.
1909, became University College, Galway, part of National University of Ireland.
Universities and colleges (Ireland)

General Prisons Board for Ireland

1235
Contempt of court (Ireland) (persons committed). A return . . . of all persons who . . . have been committed to unlimited terms of imprisonment . . . 1887-1906.
Contempt of court (Ireland);
Courts of law (Ireland)

1236
Report . . . 1-45, 1878-1922/23.
Supersedes two separate series: Di-

rectors of Convict Prisons (Ireland). Annual report . . . ; and: Inspectors of Prisons (Ireland). Report . . .
PP: 1-42, 1878-1919/20.
NP: 43-45, 1920/21-1922/23.
Prisons (Ireland)

Inspector of Inebriates Retreats, Ireland

1237
Inebriate retreats, Ireland . . . Report of the Inspector for Ireland, under the Inebriates Acts . . . 1-15, 1903/4-1918.
Drunkards and drunkenness (Ireland)

Inspector of Reformatory and Industrial Schools (Ireland)

1238
Report. 1-58, 1862-1919.
Reformatories and industrial schools (Ireland)

Inspectors of Lunatics (Ireland)

1239
Annual report . . . 1-70, 1843-1920.
PP: 1-69, 1843-1919.
NP: 70, 1920.
Lunatics and lunatic asylums II.1; Lunacy (Ireland)

Intermediate Education Board for Ireland

1240
Annual report . . . 1879-1921.
PP: 1879-1920.
NP: 1921.
Education and schools (Ireland) III.2; II.2

1241
Intermediate education (Ireland). Account . . . 1879-1921.
Education and schools (Ireland) IV.6; III.6

1242
Report . . . as to the application of the teachers' salaries grant. 1914/15-1921/22.
PP: 1914/15-1919/20.
NP: 1920/21-1921/22.
Education and schools (Ireland) II.8

1243
Rules and schedule containing the programme of examinations . . . 1902-1922.
Education and schools (Ireland) III.7

Irish Land Commission

1244
Accounts . . . 1881/82-1922/23.
Land, etc. (Ireland) IV.1(a); IV.13

1245
Evicted tenants (re-instatements). Return . . . 1907-March 1915.
1907-1908 annual, then quarterly.
Land, etc. (Ireland) IV.5

1246
Index to estates comprised in the Returns of advances . . . 1907-1919.
Land, etc. (Ireland) IV.2

1247
Irish Land Acts 1903 to 1909. Report of the Estates Commissioners . . . 1903/4-1920/21.
PP: 1903/4-1919/20.
NP: 1920/21.
Land, etc. (Ireland) III.2

1248
Judicial rents (monthly returns). Return according to provinces and counties, of judicial rents . . . 1881-1902.
Land, etc. (Ireland) IV.1(f); IV.9

1249
Purchase of Land (Ireland) Act 1891. Return of advances . . . 1891/92-1904/5.
Annual.
Later, see its: Return of advances under the Irish Land Purchase Acts . . .
Land, etc. (Ireland) IV.14(p); IV.2(a)

1250
Report of the Irish Land Commissioners. 1881/82-1920/21.
PP: 1881/82-1919/20.
NP: 1920/21.
Land, etc. (Ireland) III.3; III.1

1251

Return of advances under the Irish Land Purchase Acts . . . 1903/5-April/June 1920.

Frequency varies; generally monthly 1906-June 1915, then quarterly.

Earlier, see its: Purchase of Land (Ireland) Act 1891. Return of advances . . .

PP: 1903/5-Jan./March, 1920.
NP: April/June 1920.
Land, etc. (Ireland) IV.2(b)

1252

Return of proceedings under the Land Law Acts, the Labourers (Ireland) Acts 1883-1891, and the Land Purchases Acts . . . 1881-Feb. 1915.

Monthly from June 1882, but with many irregularities.
Land, etc. (Ireland) IV.1(n); IV.23

Land Judge's Court (Ireland)

1253

Estates in Land Judge's Court (Ireland). Return, by counties, of the estates in the Land Judge's Court, over which receivers have been appointed . . . 1904-1913.
Land, etc. (Ireland) IV.14

Local Government Board for Ireland

1254

Annual report. 1-49, 1872/73-1919/20.
Local government (Ireland) III.1

1255

Labourers cottages (Ireland). Return . . . showing the number of cottages built or in course of construction . . . 1902/3-1914/15.

Title varies.
Labour (Ireland)

1256

Labourers (Ireland). Return . . . showing the number of cottages and allotments provided under the Labourers Acts by each district council . . . 1907/8-1914/15.
Labour (Ireland)

1257

Local taxation (Ireland) returns . . . 1865-1918/19.
Local taxation (Ireland)

Lord Chancellor (Ireland)

1258

Commission of the Peace (Ireland). Return showing the names, addresses, and occupations or descriptions of the persons appointed to the Commission of the Peace . . . 1884-1914.

Title varies: Magistrates (Ireland). Return . . .
Justices (Ireland)

Lord Lieutenant (Ireland)

1259

Ireland Development Grant Act 1903. Report of proceedings . . . 1903/4-1914/15.
Development grant (Ireland)

National Health Insurance Commission (Ireland)

1260

Report . . . on the administration of national health insurance in Ireland . . . 1912/13-1917/20.

1912/13-1914/17, issued in: National Health Insurance Joint Committee. Report . . . on the administration in England . . .
Insurance, National Health III.15

Office of Treasury Remembrancer, Ireland

1261

County Officers and Courts (Ireland) Act 1877. Account . . . 1881/82-1916/17.
County courts (Ireland)

1262

National School Teachers' Pension Fund

... Account ... 1903-Jan./March 1922.
Education and schools (Ireland) III.18

Public Record Office (Ireland)

1263
Report of the Deputy Keeper of the
Public Records and Keeper of the State
Papers in Ireland ... 1-52, 1867/68-1919.
Records, public (Ireland);
Records (Ireland)

Registrar General (Ireland)

1264
Detailed annual report ... 1-58, 1864-
1921.
  PP: 1-57, 1864-1920.
  NP: 58, 1921.
Births, etc. (Ireland)

1265
Emigration statistics of Ireland ... 1876-
1920.
  Note also: Emigration statistics, Ire-
land. Return ... March 1906-Jan. 1922.
(NP)
Statistical tables III.7;
Emigration (Ireland)

1266
Judicial statistics ... 1863-1919.
Statistical tables III.12; Judicial
statistics (Ireland)

1267
Supplement to the ... Report of the
Registrar General of marriages, births
and deaths in Ireland, containing de-
cennial summaries ... 1881/90-1901/10.
Births, etc. (Ireland)

Registrar of Petty Sessions
Clerks (Ireland)

1268
Dogs Regulation (Ireland) Act 1965.
Account of the receipts and expenditure
... 1867-1914.
Dogs (Ireland)

1269
Fines, etc. (Ireland). Abstract of ac-
counts of fines accounted for by the
Registrar of Petty Sessions Clerks ...
1849/54-1913.
Fines, etc. (Ireland)

Royal Irish Constabulary

1270
Agrarian offences. Return ... 1880-
1904.
Agrarian outrages and offences
(Ireland); Judicial statistics (Ireland)

1271
Agrarian outrages. Quarterly return ...
1881-1903.
Agrarian outrages and offences
(Ireland); Judicial statistics (Ireland)

1272
Drunkenness (Ireland). Return giving
the number of arrests for drunkenness
... 1878/79-1912.
Drunkards and drunkenness (Ireland)

1273
Land Law (Ireland) Act 1887. Quarterly
returns of the number of evictions from
agricultural holdings ... July/Sept.
1889-Oct./Dec.1915.
Evictions (Ireland)

Index

References are to entry numbers, not to pages